To Denise
from Ann.

Happy Birthday!

HARRY & MEGHAN

The Royal Wedding Book

HARRY & MEGHAN

The Royal Wedding Book

Halima Sadat

PITKIN

Contents

At precisely 12 noon, the bride entered St George's Chapel through the magnificent West Door, as simply Ms Meghan Markle. The focus of all attention, she walked down the centre aisle, a picture of composure and poise, through the congregation seated in the Nave, to the entrance to the Quire where she was met by the Prince of Wales, who escorted her to the altar. Just an hour later she emerged on the arm of her husband as Her Royal Highness the Duchess of Sussex, as Prince Harry had been created Duke of Sussex (a royal Dukedom) by the Queen to mark the occasion. Meghan is now also the Countess of Dumbarton and Baroness Kilkeel. After signing the marriage register, the couple began their procession back through the Chapel. It was a magical moment and every one of the guests inside the Chapel, and indeed those watching from all over the world, was fully appreciative of the grandeur and significance of this very special occasion.

The 15th-century St George's Chapel in Windsor Castle is one of the finest ecclesiastical buildings in the land. It has been the venue for countless state and royal ceremonies throughout the centuries: marriages, funerals, and christenings of kings, queens, princes and princesses, including the baptism of Prince Harry in 1984, and of course, the annual service for the Most Noble Order of the Garter, the highest Order of Chivalry. On Saturday, 19th May 2018, another glittering and memorable chapter was written to add to this historic and illustrious list.

The wedding of Prince Harry (or to give him his full name, His Royal Highness, Prince Henry Charles Albert David of Wales) and his American fiancée, (Rachel) Meghan Markle, was a royal event with international overtones, more than a touch of glamour and glitz, and it was an entirely democratic occasion with all the elements intertwining perfectly. The invited guests at the wedding were shown to their specially allocated seats by the 25 Lay Stewards, resplendent in their morning dress and decorations. The Stewards, who act as ushers, are appointed by the Dean of Windsor, subject to the approval of the Queen, and theirs are voluntary, but nevertheless, highly sought after positions.

To ensure their privacy, the Queen and members of the royal family sat in the Quire, which they entered through the 13th-century Gilbertus Door at the side of the Chapel. They were conducted to their seats by the Gentlemen Ushers, or to give them their correct titles, Ushers-in-Ordinary. These are 10 retired senior service officers whose origins go back to the 15th century. To distinguish them from the Lay Stewards, they wear a brassard – or armband – bearing the royal cypher, and have privileged access to Her Majesty.

The Queen and the Duke of Edinburgh and the rest of the royal family occupied the Garter Stalls on the right-hand side, with Meghan's mother and guests immediately opposite. The senior Gentleman Usher handed an Order of Service to the Queen, with the only difference between hers and everyone else's was that Her Majesty's was surmounted by a small crown. As with everything organised by the Royal Household, nothing was left to chance; the day ran like clockwork with military precision, timed to the last second.

There was an outpouring of joy and affection for Harry and Meghan, as they paraded through the town after the ceremony in their open-top carriage in a two-mile procession, so everyone could get a good view. Thousands lined the streets surrounding Windsor Castle, many of whom had been there since early morning, some even days before. The couple were given the use of the beautiful Ascot Landau, built in 1883 for Queen Victoria, drawn by four of the famous Windsor Greys: Milford Haven, Storm, Plymouth and Tyrone (with Storm and Tyrone being father and son), with two outriders. Throughout Britain, numerous street parties were held to celebrate this joyous occasion. As the wedding captured attention worldwide, and an audience of over two billion royal fans tuned in to witness this most significant moment in history.

Harry and Meghan exchanged their wedding vows before the Archbishop of Canterbury, The Most Reverend Justin Welby, and the groom placed a ring made of Welsh gold on Meghan's third finger, continuing a royal wedding tradition that is ninety-five years old. The bride than placed a textured platinum band on Harry's finger. Since 1923, the wedding rings of every royal bride have been made from a single nugget of Welsh gold. It comes from a mine named Clogau St David's located at Bontddu (it means 'Black Bridge') in North Wales, and was first presented to the late Queen Mother when, as Lady Elizabeth Bowes-Lyon, she married King George V's second son, Bertie, the Duke of York (later King George VI) at Westminster Abbey in 1923.

After the ring was made, Mr Bartholomew, the mine owner, kept the rest of the gold nugget and refused to sell it to anyone else. In 1947, Princess Elizabeth was offered the gold for her wedding ring for her marriage to the then Lieutenant Commander Philip Mountbatten (now the Duke of Edinburgh). Since then, every royal bride has each had her wedding ring made from the same gold. Princess Margaret in 1960, when she married Antony Armstrong Jones (later the 1st Earl of Snowdon); Princess Anne in 1973 for her wedding to Mark Phillips; Lady Diana Spencer (the late Princess of Wales), in 1981, when she married Prince Charles; Sarah Ferguson (the Duchess of York) when she married Prince Andrew in 1986; Sophie Rhys Jones (now the Countess of Wessex) for her marriage to Prince Edward in 1999; Camilla Parker Bowles (the present Duchess of Cornwall) in 2005 when she and the Prince of Wales were married; and Catherine Middleton (now the Duchess of Cambridge) for her marriage to Prince William in 2011. As only a tiny piece of the original was left in 1981, the Royal British Legion presented the Queen with a 36-gram nugget of rare 21-carat Welsh gold. This is held by the Crown Jewellers in readiness for any future royal weddings.

Harry is sixth in line of succession to the throne so Her Majesty, as sovereign, was required to give her official approval of the marriage, which, of course, she did, and granted leave for it to take place, at a meeting of the Privy Council, when it was declared in the archaic, grandiloquent language of the Court that:

'I declare My Consent to a Contract of Matrimony between My Most Dearly Beloved Grandson Prince Henry Charles Albert David of Wales and Rachel Meghan Markle, which Consent I am causing to be signified under the Great Seal and to be entered in the Books of the Privy Council … Given at Our Court at Buckingham Palace the Fourteenth day of March 2018 in the Sixty-seventh year of Our Reign.'

Shortly before this, Meghan was baptised and confirmed into the Church of England by the Archbishop of Canterbury at a private ceremony in the Chapel Royal at St James's Palace.

There was also the question of where the wedding could take place. St George's Chapel, just like Westminster Abbey, is a 'Royal Peculiar', which means it does not come under the jurisdiction of any diocese or bishop in Britain, as most other Anglican churches do. Being a 'Royal Peculiar' indicates that the Chapel lies under the sole authority of the sovereign, so only Her Majesty was able to give permission for the ceremony to be held in St George's Chapel; which consent she was more than happy to bestow, along with her blessings and good wishes.

Harry and Meghan's relationship has developed at the pace they both desired, with Harry introducing Meghan to his family and friends gradually and making sure she was comfortable with the future demands that being royal entails. She has made light of it all, and enjoying what could have been a daunting occasion: the first meeting with the Queen. Her Majesty even broke with tradition by inviting Meghan to spend Christmas at Sandringham; the first time a fiancée had been included in what is usually an exclusive royal family occasion.

The Queen knows that to maintain the House of Windsor's longevity and durability, it is essential to welcome men and women from all walks of life without reference to race, religion or nationality. Harry was free to choose the woman he loved, and there is no doubt that with Harry and Meghan it is a love match on both sides. It was instant mutual attraction from the moment they first met, and in his case, as he later admitted, he knew immediately that 'she was the one'.

They could hardly have come from more different backgrounds. Harry was brought up in palaces and castles, educated at the most famous school in the world, Eton College, with a father who is destined to be the next king of England and a grandmother who is the longest-reigning British queen. Meghan was born into an affluent but comparatively modest family and grew up in Hollywood. She was educated privately and rose to success as an actress in a television series that is broadcast worldwide. Meghan has already proved to be very popular in Britain with her outgoing personality and warm approach to everyone she meets, while Harry gained the affection and admiration of many Americans when he completed his helicopter flying training at the Naval Air Facility in El Centro, California, and then going on to serve two tours flying Apache helicopters with the Army Air Corps in Afghanistan, alongside both British and US forces.

Meghan shares a birthday with Harry's great-grandmother, the late Queen Elizabeth, the Queen Mother: 4th August. Meghan is not the first American actress to marry a European prince; in April 1956, Grace Kelly, one of Hollywood's foremost movie stars, married His Serene Highness Prince Rainier III of Monaco and moved to live in the Royal palace in Monte Carlo.

As Meghan begins her new life, learning the unwritten but rigid rules of protocol, from this moment on, nothing will ever be the same again. Anyone, man or woman, who marries into the royal family cannot be fully prepared for the culture and class shock of becoming a member of the most famous family in the world. Every aspect of their future lives will follow a carefully pre-arranged plan. She now has her own Coat of Arms designed by the College of Arms, and a father-in-law, Prince Charles, and brother-in-law, Prince William, both destined to be future kings.

Her diary will be in the hands of her private secretary and her engagements, private and public, will be arranged many months ahead. Her days will be organised by the Royal Household and she will be surrounded by armed security bodyguards wherever she goes. A visit to the theatre or her favourite restaurant will involve advance planning by her team to make sure nothing and no one 'unsuitable' is likely to be present. If she decides she would like to drive herself with a friend, that friend will have to sit in the back seat as only her bodyguard is allowed to sit alongside her in case of emergency.

The Queen and her family accept without question the privilege and positions they occupy, as is the principle of an hereditary monarchy that has lasted for 1,000 years in Britain. Family continuity is all important, so even though Harry and Meghan are unlikely to become king and queen, their place is crucial in maintaining the stability and popularity of the monarchy as a symbol of unity throughout the land. Resilience and survival skills have kept the House of Windsor not only intact but also stronger for the past century; they take it all in their stride.

Harry and Meghan have already revealed much social concern and become involved in the problems of the under-privileged in a way that few others of their generation have displayed. They are a good team and a formidable combination of star quality and the common touch. They have revealed the generous, good-natured but pragmatic face of modern royalty and Meghan has allowed her own independent and vivacious personality to shine through the demands of royal protocol. Meghan has already had a taste of the future when she has accompanied Harry on some of his public duties – and there are thousands more to follow. As Harry's grandfather, Prince Philip, has remarked, 'It's the price we pay for the positions we occupy.'

If the couple need an example to follow in the years ahead, they need look no further than that set by the Queen, who is the very personification of diplomacy and discretion; qualities that have enabled her to carry out her public duties with flawless professionalism for more than sixty-five years. As President Ronald Reagan once put it, 'She will be a hard act to follow.'

If there was perhaps one moment of sadness for Harry during the marriage ceremony, it was that his beloved mother, the late Diana, Princess of Wales, was not present to share this, the happiest day of his life. He would have been sure that she was watching over him somewhere – in spirit, as he and Meghan set out on the great adventure of their future lives together.

Brian Hoey

PAGES 6–7: *Members of The Queen's Guard march through the streets of Windsor as the Duke and Duchess of Sussex leave for the procession in their Ascot Landau carriage*

OVERLEAF: *The personal touch: flowers adorn the front of the organ loft inside St George's Chapel, a special request from the bridge and groom*

The
Nation
Celebrates

A new member has joined the British Royal Family, one that has been described as a 'breath of fresh air' as the monarchy evolves with modern life in Britain. Meghan Markle is now part of a dynasty, with many members.

Although Buckingham Palace is the official residence of the Queen, it is Windsor Castle that holds a special place in her heart, and it is the home where she chooses to spend most of her time, particularly when 'off duty'. Set overlooking the historic town of Windsor, through which runs the River Thames, and surrounded by the Great Park, the castle offers a space of tranquillity while also being conveniently located for London, just 20 miles (32km) away.

The original castle was built as a motte and bailey (i.e. a stone keep with an enclosed courtyard erected on a mound) in the 11th century after the Norman invasion by William the Conqueror, but it has been added to and altered over the centuries by the successive monarchs who have used the castle since the reign of Henry I, each stamping their own taste and era on the building. Included within its walls is St George's Chapel, the 800-year-old church that has been the venue of numerous royal weddings over the centuries – including most recently, in 2005, the marriage blessing of Harry's father Prince Charles to Camilla Parker Bowles.

Across the river from Windsor is the small town of Eton, home of the famous Eton College where Harry and his brother William had their secondary level education, attending from the age of 13. As the school is within walking distance of the castle, the two boys often crossed the river via the bridge to visit their grandmother, the Queen, to enjoy afternoon tea with her when she was in residence.

PREVIOUS PAGE: *Crowds cheer the happy couple on the Long Walk in Windsor during the wedding celebrations on 19 May 2018*

LEFT: *An aerial view of Windsor Castle and the beautiful surrounding grounds. St George's Chapel is in the forefront, where the bride and groom exchanged their vows*

These visits, along with others as a family, make Windsor a place of significance to Harry, and indeed, more recently, he and Meghan have spent a great deal of time at the castle during the 18 months leading up to their wedding.

It is perhaps no surprise that the couple have chosen to marry in Windsor. It is a beautiful location, which holds fond memories for Harry and, also now, for his bride, and it has several other advantages. The privacy of the chapel and its relatively small size allows for a more personal and tailored ceremony. Furthermore, and importantly, its proximity to the Queen and Prince Philip's private residence in Windsor castle meant the journey to the church for Harry's now elderly grandparents was short and easy, and this would have been a major consideration when the choice of venue was made.

In preparation for her wedding, Meghan was baptised into the Anglican church in a private ceremony held at the Chapel Royal within St James's Palace and attended by Prince Charles and his wife Camilla. Meghan was brought up in a Protestant home and attended a Roman Catholic school; however, her baptism, which was followed by her confirmation, makes her a member of the Church of England, of which the Queen is the head. While not a prerequisite for her marriage in St George's Chapel, Meghan chose to be baptised as a mark of a respect to her then future grandmother-in-law the Queen. Holy water from the River Jordan is thought to have been used for the baptism, which was carried out, at Meghan's specific request, by the Archbishop of Canterbury, Justin Welby. To commemorate the special day, Meghan was seen wearing a delicate bracelet featuring a diamond cross in recognition of her baptism.

ST GEORGE'S CHAPEL

The beautiful St George's Chapel situated within the boundaries of Windsor Castle has been the church of choice for many royals for weddings over the centuries. As a member of the royal family, Harry is entitled to marry at St George's, and there have been several other royal weddings held at the chapel in recent times. In addition to the blessing of Charles and Camilla in 2005, Harry's uncle Prince Edward married Sophie Rhys-Jones in the chapel in 1999, and his cousin Peter Philips wed his Canadian wife

The Invitations

Meghan and Harry's wedding invitations were printed by the company
Barnard & Westwood, which has held the 'Royal Warrant for Printing
and Bookbinding by Appointment to Her Majesty the Queen' since 1985
and has a second royal warrant with Prince Charles. The invitations,
featuring the Three Feather Badge of the Prince of Wales, were printed
in black and gold, using American ink and English card, thereby reflecting
the nationalities of the couple. A technique of burnishing was used and
traditional wedding etiquette was followed with the invitations being
issued by Harry's father Prince Charles. There was also a modern touch as
on the listing of the couple's names, the bride was referred to as Meghan,
as she prefers to be known, rather than by her official first name of Rachel,
and was entitled Ms instead of the more usual Miss.

Autumn Kelly there in 2008. In October 2018, another of Harry's cousins, Eugenie, is to marry her fiancé Jack Brooksbank in the chapel. In fact, St George's is one of the most exclusive wedding venues in the country as, in addition to the royal family, only residents of Windsor Castle and the College of St George enjoy the privilege of marrying within this impressive building.

While its gothic architecture is ornate and impressive, the chapel provides an intimate atmosphere that would be more difficult to achieve in other venues, such as the grandiose Westminster Abbey or St Paul's Cathedral. The history of St George's dates from the 13th century when a chapel was first built on the site by Henry III, although the current building was erected by Edward III in 1337 when it was linked to the newly built College of the Order of the Garter. It was expanded by Edward IV, who had deemed it to be insufficiently grand, and further improvements were carried out by Kings Henry VII and VIII. The chapel suffered great damage in the English Civil War of the mid-17th century when the 15th-century chapter house was destroyed. During this time, there was much plundering and looting of precious objects carried out by anti-monarchy forces, known as the Roundheads, who were loyal to the 'republican' Oliver Cromwell. With Cromwell's successful takeover of the country and the execution of Charles I, there followed 11 years of rule by Parliamentarians. In 1660, the monarchy was re-established under Charles II and work was started on repairing the chapel to restore it to its former glory. Some 200 years later, Queen Victoria carried out further works that included the completion of the Lady Chapel, the construction of which had been started by Henry VII only for it to be abandoned part-built. Victoria also commissioned steps to be built at the west end of the chapel to create a spectacular ceremonial entrance to the building.

In addition to its architecture, St George's is famous for its artworks, in particular its stained-glass windows, which date from the early 16th century to modern times, and the 76 statues that represent the heraldic beasts, such as the lion of England, the dragon of Wales, the greyhound of Richmond and the falcon of York, among others. The current statues were placed on the external pinnacles in 1925 to replace the original 16th-century ones that were removed by Charles II in 1682 on the advice of the great architect Sir Christopher Wren who disliked the Reigate stone from which they had been carved.

PRINCESS ELIZABETH AND PHILIP

If Meghan and Harry were to search for role models for a long and happy marriage, Harry's own grandparents, the Queen and her husband Prince Philip, have found the recipe for a successful marriage that has lasted for seven decades.

The royal couple, who in 2017 celebrated their 70th – or platinum – wedding anniversary, have been man and wife since 20 November 1947, when Princess Elizabeth, as she was then, married the man she loved, Philip Mountbatten, at Westminster Abbey.

The wedding came in the period immediately following the end of the Second World War when the country was still recovering from the privations, damage and loss associated with the conflict. Sir Winston Churchill, who had led the country throughout the years of war, declared it to be a 'flash of colour' in the difficult times of austerity that the country was facing as it sought to rebuild itself.

While the people were happy to celebrate the event, the royal family was careful to avoid any obvious ostentation or extravagance by way of acknowledgement of the problems the country was experiencing. Indeed, fabric for the 21-year-old Princess' dress had to be paid for with ration coupons, although the government made the concession of donating her an extra 200 coupons to allow for the creation of the beautiful silk satin fit-and-flare gown with its 13-foot train by couturier Norman Hartnell. To complete the wedding outfit, Elizabeth wore a silk veil, decorated with silver star lilies and orange blossom to match the embroidery on her dress, and this was secured by a diamond tiara lent to her by her mother Queen Elizabeth (later to be the Queen Mother), a tiara that had to have an emergency repair as it snapped unexpectedly on the morning of the wedding. For Philip, his wedding ensemble presented less of a problem as he looked every inch the naval officer in his dress uniform, medals adorning his chest, complete with a ceremonial sword in his hand. The challenge was to create a wedding with the pomp and ceremony that such a state occasion required, but still with a view to economy and the need to overcome the difficulty of obtaining certain items; for example, the hard-to-source ingredients for the nine-foot-high four-tier cake were donated by the Australian Girl Guides as a tactful solution to a delicate problem.

On the day, thousands lined the streets to watch the wedding procession and be part of the joyous day. They were not disappointed as they watched the spectacle of the Princess and her father, George VI, travel in the Irish State Coach, drawn by a pair of Windsor Greys and accompanied by red-and-gold liveried coachmen as they travelled to the Abbey. Then, once again, following the service and vows in the Abbey, which were officiated by the Archbishop of Canterbury Geoffrey Fisher and the Archbishop of York Cyril Garbett, the crowds cheered in delight as they watched the newly married Princess and her husband wave from the beautiful Glass Coach on their route to Buckingham Palace for the wedding breakfast and not one, but three, balcony appearances.

PRINCE CHARLES AND CAMILLA

St George's Chapel was the venue of the wedding of Harry's father Charles when he married Camilla Parker Bowles in April 2005. The wedding had two parts, the first of which was the civil ceremony at the Guildhall set outside the castle walls within the town itself. There, the couple made their vows to each other and exchanged rings (Charles chooses to wear his, unconventionally, on the little finger of his left hand instead of the more usual third) before signing the register with Charles' son Prince William and Camilla's son Tom acting as witnesses. The idea had been for this part of the day to be low key but, nevertheless, crowds turned out to cheer Charles and his new bride as they left for the second part of their wedding, the blessing in St George's Chapel. This took the form of a service of prayer and dedication, conducted by the Archbishop of Canterbury, the Most Reverend and Right Honourable Dr Rowan Williams.

The service was attended by members of the royal family, including the Queen and Prince Philip – who had forgone the civil ceremony in order to avoid attracting too much attention – leading UK politicians, several foreign royal heads of state,

Princess Elizabeth and the Duke of Edinburgh on their wedding day on 20 November 1947

religious representatives and governors-general of Commonwealth countries, as well as family and friends.

Both Prince Charles and Camilla wore outfits that would be considered informal for a royal wedding. Charles wore a black tailcoat with grey striped trousers and a grey waistcoat, and Camilla looked radiant in two contrasting, yet simple, outfits. For the civil ceremony, she wore a cream knee-length dress and coat and for the church, she chose a floor-length blue and gold embroidered coat with a matching dress underneath. Each outfit was created by the British design house Robinson Valentine and was accessorised by a Philip Treacy hat and feather headdress respectively.

PRINCE WILLIAM AND CATHERINE

While Meghan and Harry opted for a relatively small wedding in terms of royal marriages, the same could not be said of his brother William when he married his long-time girlfriend Catherine Middleton on 29 April 2011. The wedding, which took place in Westminster Abbey, was a grand occasion as befitting a future King. Unlike St George's Chapel, which holds around 800 worshippers, the Abbey can accommodate around 2,000, and its spectacular interior makes it the church of choice for any state religious ceremony. William and Catherine managed to achieve the informal and intimate atmosphere they hoped for on their big day by the clever use of floral arrangements and a line of hornbeam and maple trees arranged along the length of the aisle to give a rustic feel that one might find in a country church.

'a grand occasion as befitting of a future king'

Harry was best man, or his 'supporter', at his brother's wedding, and the pair looked resplendent in their military dress uniforms – William in his scarlet Irish Guards colonel's uniform with a bright blue garter sash, and Harry in his

Prince Charles and Camilla Parker Bowles on their wedding day on 9 April 2005

navy-blue dress officer's uniform of the Blues and Royals. However, it was the bride, of course, who stole the day in her long-sleeved, ivory duchesse satin, hand-embroidered gown created by British designer Sarah Burton at Alexander McQueen. As Catherine arrived at her groom's side, having processed down the aisle on the arm of her father Michael, William smiled at her and said, 'You look beautiful.'

The service was largely traditional, following the 1966 Book of Common Prayer, although the couple were able to add a personal touch in the form of a special prayer they had composed for the day. Following the signing of the register, the newlyweds left the Abbey to the notes of Crown Imperial by William Walton to then pass through a guard of honour outside, made up of members of the three armed forces, with a full peal of bells ringing out in celebration.

An open landau drawn by four white horses conveyed the Duke and Duchess of Cambridge, as they were now titled, to Buckingham Palace for their reception and, of course, for that all-important balcony appearance when the newlyweds delighted the thousands of cheering onlookers with not one but two kisses. It was a spectacular day, with all the pomp and circumstance that such an important state occasion demands. Yet it was also a day, thanks to live television broadcasting from within the Abbey, that allowed the people, both in the UK and the Commonwealth – and indeed across the world – to share in William and Catherine's joy and witness the creation of a royal union based on true love and mutual respect.

Prince William and Catherine share a kiss on the balcony of Buckingham Palace in front of millions of well-wishers on their wedding day on 29 April 2011

HANDS ACROSS THE OCEAN

Fans of the royal family on both sides of the Atlantic will have been celebrating the marriage, as will those who follow Meghan and Harry as individuals. Similarly, Canada, which is an original member of the Commonwealth and has a particular affection for Meghan, will have joined its neighbour to the south by rejoicing in the wedding. As has been emphasised by current prime minister Theresa May and her predecessor David Cameron, the United Kingdom has always enjoyed a special relationship with the United States and this will, no

'the British monarchy has come of age'

doubt, be enhanced by the royal couple's union. The marriage will have raised the profile of both Meghan and Harry within the North American continent and as these countries are both major world economies with huge influence, they can do much to help the newlyweds spread their messages far and wide.

In recent times Harry has formed a strong bond with former US President Barack Obama, who helped the prince launch the Invictus Games in Toronto. When Harry acted as guest editor on BBC 4's *Best of Today*, it was Barack he chose to interview, during which it was clear the two men enjoy mutual respect and friendship. With their shared enthusiasm for helping young people achieve their potential, it is a relationship that will continue to grow. Similarly, Barack's wife Michelle shares Meghan's interest in gender and racial equality, thereby representing another way the couple might work together in the future.

By marrying Meghan, Harry has moved the royal family into the modern world, one in which nationality, colour and background play no part. No longer will senior members of the royal family be constrained in their choice of spouse, as had previously been the case, even in relatively recent times. It could be said that the British monarchy has come of age.

Hand-in-hand, Prince Harry and Meghan emerge through the West Door of St George's Chapel on their wedding day on 19 May 2018

A
Royal
Wedding

Saturday 19 May 2018 dawned warm, sunny and calm and as it did a tangible sense of excitement rippled through the early crowds who had gathered on Windsor's streets to join in the celebrations for Harry and Meghan's big day. Many had camped out overnight, or even longer, to be sure of securing a good vantage point from which to watch the newlyweds process through the city's streets and to wave and cheer as they passed by.

Windsor itself had been preparing for the day for several weeks, with 1,000 metres of bunting flying – some of it made by the schoolchildren of Windsor and the surrounding county of Berkshire – shop windows were specially decorated and barriers and viewing stands for crowds and media erected. Preparations included fresh tarmac on roadways, weed removal from green areas and new coats of paint for signs and selected buildings. As for everything else in the town, if it could be washed and cleaned then it was, right down to lampposts, windows, walls and the streets themselves. Windsor was ready!

As with all royal weddings, everything was timed to perfection, and to help things run to plan, rehearsals had been the order of the day, not only in St George's Chapel for the couple themselves but also for everyone associated with the wedding, to include a mock-up of the carriage procession through the town. Nothing was left to chance to make sure that the day would run like clockwork.

Some 600 guests were invited to the ceremony in the chapel and the lunch reception in St George's Hall, with 200 of Meghan's friends attending the evening party afterwards in Frogmore House, Windsor. In the chapel, closest friends and family members were seated in the medieval quire, while the rest of the congregation were in the nave, the groom's guests to the right and the bride's to the left. As expected, the guests included celebrities from the more glamorous side of the couple's life, as well as those who share the same interests and passions as the bride and groom, one of whom was Lawrence Munro, a south African conservationist who once saved a group of visitors to a national park from an angry rhino. Prince Seeiso of Lesotho, with whom Harry set up the charity Sentebale, and Sentebale ambassador Ignacio Figueras were also honoured guests, as were representatives of the many charities and foundations supported by the couple.

Celebrity guests included many of Meghan's dearest friends, such as the American tennis star Serena Williams, Indian actress Priyanka Chopra, stylist Jessica Mulroney and fashion designer Misha Nonoo. Also invited to take part in the celebrations within the castle walls, and first to arrive of the guests, were 2,640 members of the public, a gesture that was also a part of the marriage of Harry's uncle Prince Edward and his wife Sophie Rhys-Jones who married at St George's Chapel in 1999. Of those gathered in the part of the Castle known as the Lower Ward, 1,200 were young people from a wide range of backgrounds selected by nine regional Lord Lieutenant offices for the strong leadership and exceptional service they had demonstrated within their local community. Also present were a number of survivors of the Manchester Arena attack in May 2017 and the Grenfell Tower fire in June of that same year.

Other guests included 200 people who work for a number of charities and organisations, such as WellChild and the Invictus Games, 100 pupils from two local schools (the Royal School in Windsor Great Park and St George's School near the castle itself), 610 community members of Windsor Castle and 530 members the Royal Household and the Crown Estate.

Notable by their absence were heads of state from countries around the world, religious leaders, political figures and dignitaries. Harry's marriage to Meghan was considered to be very much a personal, private celebration, paid for by the Royal Family itself, rather than a grand State occasion, and therefore it was deemed inappropriate to invite guests with no direct connection to the royal couple. However, former prime minister Sir John Major was present by virtue of his personal connection to the couple and his status as a Knight of the Garter.

There was a distinct order for the arrival of guests, with friends and others entering first at the west entrance, to be followed by members of the Royal Family, who entered through the Galilee Porch. Last to arrive was the Queen herself, whose arrival was announced with a fanfare from the State Trumpeters. She was accompanied by her husband Prince Philip, who at the age of nearly 97, had only one month previously undergone a hip replacement operation.

RIGHT: *Amal Clooney wowed the crowds in an iconic Stella McCartney Goldenrod gown*

BOTTOM: *Oprah Winfrey looked glamorous in her pale pink dress, complete with vintage Philip Treacy hat*

FAR RIGHT: *Victoria and David Beckham arrive hand-in-hand to the ceremony, looking very chic and stylish*

RIGHT: *Meghan's* Suits *co-star Gina Torres looked sensational in a red lace gown*

LEFT: *Sir Elton John, who was a close friend of Harry's mother Princess Diana through her work related to HIV/AIDS awareness, cancelled two concerts in Las Vegas that had been scheduled for the weekend of the wedding.*

ABOVE LEFT: *David Henson MBE, British parasport athlete involved behind the scenes at the Invictus Games, is among the guests at the Royal Wedding*

ABOVE RIGHT: *Earl Spencer arrives at his nephew's wedding with his wife Countess Spencer*

BOTTOM RIGHT: *Victoria Aitken (third from left) and her children Lady Eliza Spencer, Louis Spencer, Viscount Althorp and Lady Kitty Spencer arrive at St George's Chapel for the wedding of their cousin*

TOP LEFT: *Idris Elba and fiancée Sabrina Dhowre are all smiles as they arrive to support Harry and Meghan on their big day*

TOP: *James Corden and his wife Julia Carey arrive for the service in Windsor before he hosted the reception at Frogmore House*

LEFT: *Serena Williams accessorised her Versace dress with a pale pink fascinator*

ABOVE: *Pretty in pink; the Duchess of Cornwall completes her outfit with a spectacular hat by Philip Treacy. She is shown here arriving with her husband the Prince of Wales*

RIGHT: *The mother of the bride, Doria, looked elegant in a pistachio green dress and coat by Oscar de la Renta*

ABOVE: *The Duke of York arrives with his daughters Princesses Eugenie (left) and Beatrice (right)*

LEFT: *The Earl and Countess of Wessex wave to cheering crowds with their daughter Lady Louise Windsor and son James, Viscount Severn*

ABOVE: *Happily the Duke of Edinburgh was able to attend his grandson's wedding, after recovering from a recent hip operation*

RIGHT: *Her Majesty the Queen wore a seasonal, flared dress and coat by Stewart Parvin*

RIGHT: *Harry beams as he arrives with his brother and best man, the Duke of Cambridge*

As Harry stood nervously at the altar awaiting his bride, alongside his brother and best man William, he might have reflected for a moment on the fact that his marriage was another significant piece in the jigsaw of St George's Chapel's 1,000-year history. The two men also might have recalled William's own wedding in Westminster Abbey seven years previously, when the roles were reversed and Harry was best man – a situation that now, Harry joked, allowed him to get his 'revenge' on his brother.

At William's wedding, Harry had worn a navy captain's dress uniform of the Blues and Royals, while William, as groom, had stood out in the scarlet tunic of the Irish Guards. On this occasion, Harry's day, the brothers matched each other in the formal frock coat major's uniform with red-striped navy/black trousers of the Blues and Royals, complete with white sash and gloves, and each featuring flying brevets to denote a pilot. William also wore his Garter star, reflecting his status as an aide-de-camp to the Queen, and the gold braiding of the Queen's cypher, known as an aiguillette, while Harry displayed four medals; one for the KCVO, one with a rosette for his tour to Afghanistan, along with one each for the Queen's Diamond and Golden Jubilees. The uniforms were tailored by Dege & Skinner of Savile Row. As the brothers had walked together prior to making their entrance through the West door, they had been wearing the accompanying navy caps, trimmed with red and blue, but these were removed once inside the chapel.

Harry had, somewhat controversially, chosen to retain his beard for the day, another indication that both he and his bride had been determined to do things their way. As it is customary to be clean-shaven when in army uniform, Harry had to obtain special permission from the Queen.

The little ones nearly stole the show in their adorable outfits; the bridesmaids in simple white dresses accessorised by floral headbands and mini bouquets to match that of the bride, and the pageboys complementing Harry's military uniform.

Pre-wedding nerves; Harry gazes down the aisle ahead of the arrival of his bride-to-be

In total, Meghan had in attendance, from both sides of the Atlantic, four pageboys and six bridesmaids, with ages ranging from seven to two, to give an average age of just under five. Two familiar faces featured in the group, those of Prince George, aged four, and Princess Charlotte, aged three, both of whom had performed this important duty before when, in 2017, they attended the wedding of their aunt Pippa Middleton, the sister of their mother. However, their baby brother Prince Louis did not put in an appearance, as at only three weeks old, he was deemed too young to take part in the celebrations.

Other children included from Harry's side were his three-year-old goddaughter Florence van Cutsem (daughter of Major Nicholas and Alice van Cutsem), Zalie Warren, aged two, another goddaughter of Harry's (daughter of Zoe and Jake Warren), and his godson Jasper Dyer aged six (son of Amanda and Mark Dyer MVO). From Meghan's side, the children were sons and daughters of close friends, namely Remi and Ryan Litt, aged six and seven respectively (daughters of Meghan's close friends Benita and Darren Litt), and the three Mulroney children, four-year old Ivy and seven-year-old twins Brian and John, the daughter and sons of Jessica and Benedict Mulroney. Jessica, who works as a stylist, is a particularly close friend of Meghan's and assisted with much of the wedding preparations and planning.

Meghan made the decision not to have a maid of honour as, with so many close friends, she felt she could not choose one over another. Instead, her train was ably carried and adjusted by the Mulroney twins, who repeated their important role as Meghan left the chapel after the ceremony. Having first been organised by Catherine, the Duchess of Cambridge, and George's nanny Maria, the children followed the bride down the aisle as is the British custom. Apart from one brief tearful moment on the part of one bridesmaid, all were impeccably behaved throughout what must have seemed to them an overwhelming occasion.

Princess Charlotte, Ivy Mulroney and Florence Van Cutsem wave confidently to cheering crowds as they arrive with one of the pageboys, Prince George, and the Duchess of Cambridge and Jessica Mulroney

At royal weddings, timing is perfect to the minute and so it was that at 11.59am, exactly as had been meticulously planned, Meghan arrived at the steps of St George's Chapel, having travelled there by car, a sparkling 1950s Rolls-Royce Phantom IV, from the Cliveden House Hotel, where she had spent the night, accompanied by her mother Doria. Meghan, keen to involve both her parents, had hoped that her father, Thomas, would walk her down the aisle to give her away and the intention had been for a handover from one parent to the other on arriving at the chapel. Sadly, this was not to be as Thomas was unable to attend his youngest child's wedding due to ill health and, instead, he was reported to have watched the ceremony on television from California. As a result of this unexpected change of plan, Doria left the car to take her place in the chapel quire ahead of Meghan's arrival, where she sat as the only member of the bride's family.

As she stepped out of the car, accompanied by pageboys Brian and John Mulroney, Meghan's arrival was announced by the State Trumpeters with a fanfare written specially for the occasion. At that moment and seeing the dress for the first time, the crowd outside cheered their approval, while those inside, not least of all Harry, awaited excitedly for her to make her first appearance.

Meghan's bouquet was an example of understated elegance. Small and natural in design, like the church flowers, it was designed by Philippa Craddock, but with the added touch that some of the flowers were personally handpicked by Harry from the couple's private garden at Kensington Palace. Among the flowers were forget-me-nots, the favourite flower of Harry's late mother Princess Diana, specifically selected as a way of including her in the celebrations. Other flowers making up the bouquet were sweet peas, lily of the valley, astilbe, jasmine and astrantia.

Also, in Meghan's bouquet was a sprig of myrtle, a flower which symbolises marriage and love. Sourced from the garden of Osborne House on the Isle of Wight, myrtle has traditionally featured in royal bouquets since the marriage of Queen Victoria's eldest daughter, Victoria. The original plant was brought to England from Germany where it was given to Queen Victoria by the grandmother of her husband Prince Albert. Similar mini bouquets were carried by the bridesmaids, which, like Meghan's, were bound in naturally dyed raw silk ribbon.

As Meghan drove on her route to the chapel in the Rolls-Royce, onlookers had a tiny glimpse of what her dress was to be like, but it wasn't until she stepped out of the car, that it was revealed in its full glory, the dress that had been the subject of much speculation as to the designer and style.

The dress proved to be simple in design – made from double-bonded silk cady with an underskirt of triple silk organza. It was designed by Clare Waight Keller, the first ever female artistic director at the French fashion house Givenchy. The unadorned gown featured a wide boatneck and three-quarter-length sleeves, making an elegant style statement of pared-down chic, through soft tailoring and immaculate cut, that was in contrast to the beautifully embellished engagement gown by Ralph & Russo that Meghan had selected for her official engagement photos.

To offset the dress, Meghan wore a spectacular lace-edged silk tulle veil, 16 feet (five metres) in length and adorned with embroidered floral emblems representing the 53 countries of the Commonwealth; countries where she and Harry, following their marriage, will spend much time working over the coming years. Also included in the clever design, as a personal touch, were Meghan's favourite flowers of wintersweet, found in the gardens of Kensington Palace, and the Californian poppy of her homeland. Each hand-embroidered flower was unique, thereby creating a very special veil that was not only symbolic but also extremely beautiful.

With Meghan's hair tied up in an elegant chignon, the veil was held in place by the Order of Splendour tiara that once belonged to Queen Mary, wife of King George V. The platinum tiara, lent to Meghan by the Queen, is in a bandeau art deco style, popular at the time of its making in 1932. Comprised of 11 sections, it is heavily decorated with diamonds and features a central detachable brooch, containing 10 diamonds, that was originally given to Queen Mary on her marriage to the then Prince George, Duke of York. To complement the tiara, Meghan wore simple diamond earrings and a bracelet by top jewellers Cartier. Meghan completed her outfit with co-ordinating silk duchesse satin pointed shoes, also from Givenchy.

TOP: *Meghan on her way to the chapel with her mother Doria in a 1950s vintage Rolls-Royce Phantom IV*

RIGHT: *The moment the world has been waiting for. The radiant bride arrives at St George's Chapel, her dress and veil glinting in the May sunshine*

In the absence of her father, Meghan took the brave decision to enter the chapel alone, walking calmly and confidently to the accompaniment of a beautiful solo performance of Handel's 'Eternal Source of Light Divine' sung by Welsh soprano Elin Manahan. As she reached the organ screen, she was joined by Prince Charles who escorted her to her groom's side, a sure sign that Meghan has been fully and fondly accepted by Harry's family. While it is unusual for a man other than the bride's father to give her away, this was, in fact, a duty Charles had performed once before, despite having no daughters, as in 2016, on her wedding day, he escorted Alexandra Knatchbull, daughter of Lord and Lady Brabourne, when her father Norton, a close friend of Charles, was too ill to carry out the task.

For Charles, who had been pleased to accept Meghan's request to stand in for her own father, the moment no doubt held special significance as it was in this same chapel that he and his wife Camilla had had their marriage blessed some 13 years earlier, in April 2005. As Meghan and Charles approached the high altar, Harry turned to mouth the words, 'Thank you, Pa,' to be followed by, 'You look amazing – I missed you,' to a beaming Meghan as she stepped to his side. As Harry lifted and arranged his bride's veil, Meghan's face was revealed, lightly made up with the freckles that she refuses to conceal clearly on view.

The ceremony began with the greeting by the Dean of Windsor David Connor, who welcomed the congregation and gave a moving reminder of the meaning behind marriage and its importance to the individuals involved and the community beyond. This was followed by the first hymn, 'Lord of All Hopefulness' and the declarations led by the Archbishop of Canterbury Justin Welby. While Harry and Meghan, as expected, agreed to their own declarations, an unusual and touching addition was a declaration made by the congregation vowing to support and uphold the couple in the marriage through the unanimous response, 'we will'.

Following the collect by the Archbishop, Lady Jane Fellowes, Harry's aunt and sister of his mother Diana, gave a reading from the Song of Solomon, after which the choir of St George's performed a beautiful arrangement of the song 'If Ye Love Me' by Thomas Tallis. For this part of the service, the couple and congregation had taken their seats and Meghan's spectacular train stretched along the aisle.

The image of confidence and grace; Meghan walks by herself down the aisle of the
nave in St George's Chapel, behind the Dean of Windsor and followed by her ten
bridesmaids and pageboys

THIS SPREAD: *The Prince of Wales accompanies his future daughter-in-law to the end of the quire and hands her to his son, a warm and symbolic welcome to the royal family. Harry, filled with awe and emotion, greets his bride by saying, 'you look amazing – I missed you'*

PREVIOUS PAGES: *As Harry removes Meghan's veil, Queen Mary's diamond bandeau tiara, made in 1932 and lent to her by The Queen, sparkles in the light*

RIGHT: *The service was led by The Right Reverend David Conner KCVO, Dean of Windsor*

Then came one of the more unorthodox moments when the Most Reverend Michael Curry took to the pulpit to give the address. Reverend Curry is the first African-American to be elected as presiding bishop and primate of the Episcopal Church in America and he has expressed strong views on discrimination relating to race and sexual orientation. A highly charismatic speaker, unsurprisingly, he gave an animated, powerful and moving address on the subject of love with a message drawn from the Song of Solomon and opening words quoted from race activist Martin Luther King. In keeping with the American theme and by way of another break with tradition, there followed a stirring performance of the Ben E. King song 'Stand by Me' by gospel singers the Kingdom Choir led by Karen Gibson, before the vows were taken. These followed the marriage service from the Common Worship 2000 with the word 'you' replacing 'thee' and 'thou' and 'cherish' in place of 'obey'.

With Harry and Meghan having made their vows, it was time for the next important moment, that of the exchange of the rings – blessed by the Archbishop – to symbolise the couple's union. As each looked into the other's eyes, the traditional words declaring commitment were spoken as the rings, made by Cleave and Company of London, were gently pushed onto third fingers of left hands. While Meghan's ring was a simple gold band made of Welsh gold as is the tradition for royalty, Harry, once more breaking with tradition, chose to wear a textured platinum design, thereby making him the only man in his immediate family to wear a wedding ring – neither Prince Philip nor Prince William wear a ring, and Prince Charles wears a gold signet ring on his little finger.

With rings in place, the proclamation was given by the Archbishop, during which, at precisely 12.40pm, Harry and Meghan were declared husband and wife. At that point, the crowds outside, who had been watching the proceedings on a large screen, erupted in cheers of jubilation so loud, they could clearly be heard inside the chapel.

The service drew to a close with the marriage blessing, prayers from the Reverend Prebendary Rose Hudson-Wilkin and Archbishop Angaelos of the Coptic Church, and the congregation joining in the hymn 'Guide Me, O Thou Great Redeemer', before the Dean of Westminster blessed everyone present.

The newlyweds could now leave the main part of the chapel to enter a side room for the legal signing of the register, Prince Charles and Meghan's mother Doria acting as the witnesses.

While the register was being signed, the guests were treated to a wonderful musical experience, when cello prodigy Sheku Kanneh-Mason performed one solo and two accompanied pieces, starting with 'Sicilienne' by Maria Theresia von Paradis, to be followed by 'Après un Rêve' by Gabriel Fauré and ending with the haunting and popular 'Ave Maria' by Franz Schubert. Sheku, who had appeared on *Britain's Got Talent* in 2015 and was winner of the BBC's Young Musician of the Year contest in 2016, had been specially asked to perform by Meghan.

Indeed, from the arrival in the chapel, the congregation had enjoyed a series of pieces played by an orchestra comprised of members of the National Orchestra of Wales, the English Chamber Orchestra and the Philharmonia, conducted by Christopher Warren-Green. The music, which Prince Charles had assisted Harry and Meghan in selecting, had a distinctly English theme, featuring composers such as Sir Edward Elgar, Ralph Vaughan Williams, Herbert Howells and Sir Alfred Herbert Brewer. All music for the service was overseen by James Vivien, the director of music for St George's Chapel. Finally, came the procession of the bride and groom as they left the chapel – pausing briefly to curtsey and bow to the Queen as they passed by – to the sound of the orchestra playing 'Symphony No. 1 in B Flat' by William Boyce, then to be greeted outside by the Kingdom Choir joyfully singing Etta James' 'Amen (This Little Light of Mine)'.

Doria, who had sat alone during the service and had looked emotional at times, left the chapel beaming and clearly delighted for her daughter, as she was escorted arm-in-arm by Prince Charles and his wife Camilla, evidence of her warm acceptance into the family. There followed her first photograph as mother of the bride, standing alongside Prince William and Catherine, as well as the Queen herself, whom she had only met for the first time on the previous day when they took tea together.

OVERLEAF: *The Duke and Duchess of Sussex leave the chapel hand-in-hand, followed by the bridal party and proud senior members of the Royal Family*

The heady scent of spring flowers greeted the bride and groom as they emerged from the chapel. The beautiful displays in both St George's Chapel and St George's Hall were created under the direction of London-based floral designer Philippa Craddock and featured white and cream seasonal blooms, including roses, peonies, lily of the valley and foxgloves gathered from the gardens of the Crown Estate and Windsor Great Park, thereby adding a personal touch. The flowers were intertwined with beech, birch and hornbeam to create a rustic, romantic feel that softened yet blended beautifully with the dramatic interior of the chapel, which is characterised by medieval heraldic banners, ornate wood carving and exquisite stained-glass windows.

Reflecting Meghan and Harry's interest in conservation and the natural world, the flowers chosen were not only from a sustainable source but among them were also pollinator-friendly blooms, having been selected from plants in the Royal Parks' wildflower meadows that support bee populations, creatures that have suffered from considerable decline across the UK in recent years.

Meghan's love of flowers is well-known. She had described peonies, in particular, as making her 'endlessly happy'. As a single woman, she regularly treated herself to flower purchases for display around her home and, as such, she was very much involved in the design and composition of the floral arrangements for her wedding day. Working closely with the self-taught Philippa, whose talent has led her to being commissioned in the past by leading fashion houses such as Alexander McQueen and Christian Dior, as well as British Vogue and Kensington Palace, Meghan was clear in her vision for her wedding flowers and the results were spectacular as the displays climbed around doorways, up the wall to the organ loft and down the chapel staircase to produce an effect akin to an English country cottage.

Following the wedding, the arrangements were distributed to various charitable organisations and, in keeping with royal tradition, Meghan's bouquet was placed on the Tomb of the Unknown Warrior in Westminster Abbey.

Man and wife; the newlyweds emerge on the steps of the West Door to the deafening cheer of the crowds

As the happy couple left the chapel, the British State Trumpeters, clad in their distinctive red tunics and bearskin hats, performed a celebratory fanfare. The Household Cavalry also supplied the Captain's Escort with immaculately turned out horses and riders from the Mounted Regiment to accompany the bride and groom on their procession.

The 'balcony kiss', referencing the famous balcony at Buckingham Palace, is a tradition started by Harry's parents Charles and Diana at their wedding in 1981 and it is now the much-awaited moment at the end of any royal wedding ceremony at which the public are in attendance. With no suitable balcony, the top of the chapel's dramatic steps was the ideal alternative location for that very special first kiss as husband and wife, to the delight of the crowds in the Lower Ward and those outside the Castle walls watching the ceremony on screens.

To make sure that the people who had come to Windsor to celebrate the day – an incredible 120,000 of them – could have the opportunity to glimpse the couple first-hand for themselves, Harry and Meghan climbed into the open Ascot Landau coach pulled by four Windsor Greys, Harry entering first in order to assist his new wife, to start the much-anticipated procession through the town's streets. After the success of the first kiss, a second one followed, again to much delight on the part of the cheering crowd.

For every bride and groom, the wedding photos provide a special memento of a wonderful day and Harry and Meghan's beautiful photos were taken by leading photographer Alexi Lubomirski, who is also a member of the Polish aristocracy, a hereditary prince and bears the title of His Serene Highness. He is a protégé of leading photographer Mario Testino, who was a favourite of Harry's mother Princess Diana and famous for creating a series of iconic images of her. Mr Lubomirski who has photographed many A-list celebrities, such as Nicole Kidman, Beyoncé, Gwyneth Paltrow and Scarlett Johansson, took the official photographs for Harry and Meghan's engagement, combining in them intimacy and informality with glamour and romance. He shares with Harry and Meghan an interest in helping others less fortunate and he recently donated proceeds from a book he wrote on the subject of 'princely behaviour' to a charity which works to eliminate extreme poverty across the globe.

The Duke and Duchess of Sussex seal their love with a kiss

The stunning flowers that adorn the archway of the West Door perfectly showcase Harry and Meghan's personal touch

The Duke and Duchess exchange a loving look as they descend the steps; the sunlight capturing the beauty and delicacy of the long train

LEFT: *Part of the family; Charles escorts Meghan's mother Doria and his wife Camilla down the chapel steps*

RIGHT: *William keeps a watchful eye on Prince George as they depart for a well-deserved family party*

BOTTOM: *Charlotte with her delighted mother Catherine showing her ease with royal etiquette*

The Procession

The ecstatic well-wishers lining the streets
cheered in jubilation, waving Union Flags – with
the occasional American 'Stars and Stripes' and
Canadian Maple leaf also to be seen – and banners
bearing messages of congratulations, as the
newlyweds, looking relaxed, extremely happy and
accompanied by the mounted Household Cavalry
escort, passed on their procession route around
the town of Windsor.

From the castle, the carriage proceeded down
Castle Hill to the High Street and Kings Road,
before eventually turning into the wide,
tree-lined parkland avenue in the Great Park,
stretching for two and a half miles (4km) and
known as The Long Walk, to head back to the
Castle. There, with the chapel's bells ringing out
in celebration, the couple left the coach for a
photo session in the Castle's private garden to be
followed by the reception luncheon in St George's
Hall, hosted by the Queen.

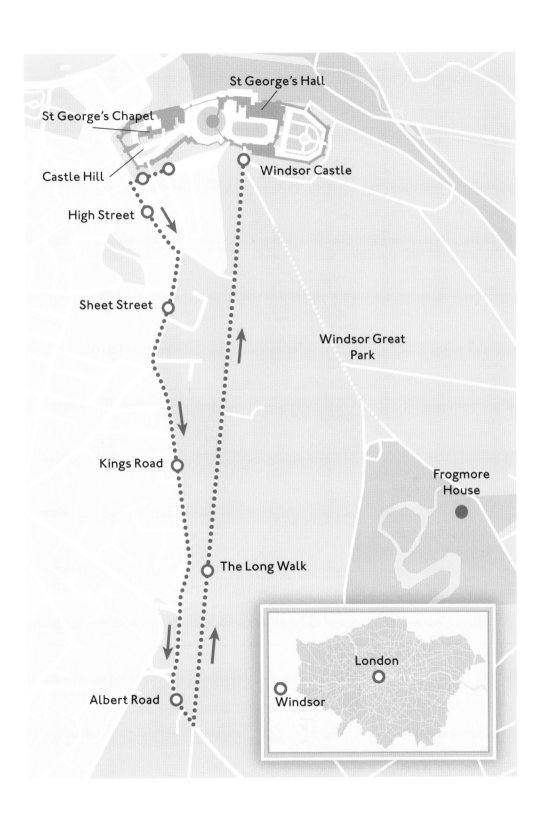

St George's Hall

St George's Chapel

Castle Hill

Windsor Castle

High Street

Sheet Street

Windsor Great Park

Kings Road

Frogmore House

The Long Walk

London

Windsor

Albert Road

RIGHT: *Meghan beams with happiness as she waves to the delighted crowd*

OVERLEAF: *The beautiful Ascot Landau built in 1883 for Queen Victoria, drawn by four of the famous Windsor Greys with two further outriders*

PAGES 86–87: *The procession winds around Windsor Castle to the jubilant cheers of the crowd*

The reception buffet lunch featured a seasonal and inventive menu created by head chef Mark Flanagan and his team of 25 and included a wide range of canapés. Guests were able to enjoy a variety of delicacies such as grilled English asparagus wrapped in Cumbrian ham, croquette confit of Windsor lamb with roasted vegetables and shallot jam, 10-hour slow-roasted Windsor pork belly with apple compote and crackling, and pea and mint risotto with pea shoots, truffle oil and Parmesan crisps, all served in easy-to-carry bowls rather than on plates to encourage the mingling of guests.

Sweet canapés included Champagne and pistachio macarons, orange crème brulée tartlets and miniature rhubarb crumble tartlets. And, of course, there was also the spectacular and unusual sponge wedding cake, made with 200 Amalfi lemons and 10 bottles of elderflower cordial.

Champagne, wine and soft drinks were on offer and, in particular, a special apple and elderflower non-alcoholic cocktail containing the same elderflower syrup used in Harry and Meghan's wedding cake and made from elderflowers sourced from the Sandringham estate.

Musical entertainment at the reception was provided by Sir Elton John, who, at Harry's request, sang three songs, one of which was the 1971 song 'Tiny Dancer' that he dedicated to the bride. Sir Elton was a good friend of Harry's mother Diana and has remained close to the family over the years since her death. Harry gave a speech in which he referred to 'my wife and I'. Prince Charles also gave an emotional speech that ended with the words, 'My darling old Harry, I'm so happy for you.'

Later, in the early evening, Harry and Meghan left Windsor Castle for Frogmore House on the Windsor Estate – Meghan now wearing a slim-fitting white halter-neck gown by British designer Stella McCartney and nude mesh shoes from Aquazurra of Mayfair. Harry drove Meghan in a silver-blue open-top E-type Jaguar with registration number E190518, reflecting the date of their special day.

Meghan's speech was reserved for the evening reception held at Frogmore, where a more intimate sit-down dinner, followed by dancing, hosted by the Prince of Wales and with Prince William as compère was enjoyed by a select 200 guests.

The Wedding Cake

Harry and Meghan's beautiful four-tier wedding cake was created by Claire Ptak, a Californian pastry chef and owner of Violet Bakery. To reflect spring, the non-traditional, organic cake was flavoured with lemon and elderflower blossom and featured Claire's signature design of fresh flowers. The cake was decorated with pale pink Swiss elderflower meringue buttercream, along with 50 fresh flowers that included peonies and roses. The cake was too heavy to stack so it was presented resting on large golden goblets. Prior to her engagement, Meghan was already familiar with the London-based bakery, having written about the 'delightful treats' produced by its kitchen on her lifestyle blog *The Tig*. The couple chose Claire not only for her delicious and beautiful cakes, but also because she shares their ethos of using only seasonal and sustainable produce with an ethical provenance.

Following the trend set by Harry's brother William and his wife Catherine when they married, Harry and Meghan opted for guests to give financial donations to a selection of charities in lieu of the more traditional wedding gifts. While the bride and groom have had no direct links with the charities selected, the issues supported by those charities reflect Harry and Meghan's interests, to include homelessness, HIV, gender equality, conservation, the armed forces and sport. Seven charities were chosen: CHIVA, which supports children in the UK living with HIV; the Myna Mahila Foundation that teaches life skills to poor women in Mumbai; Scotty's Little Soldiers which works with children who have lost a parent serving in the British armed forces; Crisis, the national charity that helps homeless people rebuild their lives; StreetGames which encourages young people and communities to become healthier and safer through sport; Surfers Against Sewage that works to protect the marine environment and its creatures; and the Wilderness Foundation UK, which teaches vulnerable teenagers living in cities about the countryside and rural employment. Several of the charities are small, with only a few employees, and for them, in particular, both the financial gift itself and the publicity associated with it have provided an enormously positive contribution to their work.

From the Queen came a more intangible gift, that of not one but three titles. As with William and Catherine, who became the Duke and Duchess of Cambridge following their wedding, Harry was bestowed the dukedom of Sussex, thereby making him HRH the Duke of Sussex and, by virtue of their marriage, Meghan HRH the Duchess of Sussex. In addition, Harry was given the titles of Earl of Dumbarton – and Meghan, therefore, Countess of Dumbarton – and Baron of Kilkeel, Meghan becoming Baroness of Kilkeel, thereby reflecting Scotland and Northern Ireland respectively.

As a commoner, Meghan will not be entitled to use the title Princess, other than formally through reference to her husband as Princess Henry of Wales, but any children she might have with Harry, due to their royal blood, will be eligible to take the status of prince or princess.

The day, although not a state occasion, was nevertheless an example of British pageantry at its best. The calm weather with clear blue skies and warm but not too hot temperatures, merely added to the success of the proceedings, even though beyond the control of any wedding organiser. Everything proceeded like clockwork, precision timing was adhered to, every detail was perfect, while the wedding itself was a wonderful combination of the traditional and the modern, the orthodox and the unexpected.

This special couple, through their warmth and humanity, have captured the hearts not only of the people of Britain but of those worldwide, with over two billion people across the globe tuning in to watch, across time zones, the live broadcasts of the entire wedding from start to finish, filmed by multinational television stations. Not least of these were Americans, in particular those in California and Meghan's home town of Los Angeles, where wedding parties starting in the early hours of the morning, accompanied by typically British food, were the order of the day.

The wide smiles on the faces of Meghan and Harry throughout the ceremony showed not only how much they were enjoying their special day, but also the depth of love they feel for each other; a love that can be summed up in Harry's words on his engagement, 'I choose her and she chooses me and whatever we have to tackle, we tackle it together.' One thing is certain, however; now as a married couple, they will achieve great things.

LEFT: *The happy couple leave hand-in-hand for their reception at Frogmore House*

ABOVE: *Harry drives his bride to their reception in an electric Jaguar*

A
Royal
Love Story

Harry and Meghan's love story began some two years before their wedding day when the couple were introduced by a mutual friend; appropriately, with Meghan's acting background, it was a meeting that would not have looked out of place in a Hollywood romance. At the time, May 2016, Meghan was based in Toronto where she was one of the stars in the television legal drama *Suits*, and Harry was visiting the city to launch the Invictus Games, the sporting event for disabled athletes that he had helped to set up.

With them both in the same location, the friend – whom the couple have declined to name – sensing that Harry and Meghan might get along, decided to do a little matchmaking and she set the pair up on a blind date. Meghan, who confessed to knowing very little about the royal family at that time, had only one question for her friend – nevertheless, for her, a very important one: 'Is he nice?' In Meghan's view, it was essential that her date should be a kind man, if she was to spend a worthwhile evening with him. Fortunately, the response was affirmative and so the two met up for a drink.

Meghan, as an American, knew very little about Prince Harry, but neither did Harry have any knowledge of her, having never seen the television show *Suits*. As a result, at this first meeting, neither had any preconceptions of what to expect from the other, something that Harry in particular found refreshing as it meant they could get to know each other as people rather than as 'celebrities' with established public images. The time flew by during that first meeting and both found themselves thinking, 'I would like to see this person again.'

PREVIOUS PAGE: *The royal couple beam with joy in the Sunken Garden of Kensington Palace after announcing their engagement*

RIGHT: *Harry and Meghan share a joke during their first official engagement together at the Nottingham Academy in December 2017*

It soon became clear that they felt at ease with one another and had a huge amount in common – so much so that they decided to meet again the following day. There was a clear spark between the two and, again, the date went well. It was then that Harry, now completely smitten, took a chance and asked Meghan to join him for a few days' holiday, an unusual offer that he considered a 'huge leap' after only two dates, but one he hoped she would accept.

Harry was due to travel to Botswana as part of a team involved in elephant translocation. It is a country that he loves, where he feels 'plugged into the earth' and free to be himself and, not surprisingly, he was keen to share its wonderful sights, sounds and smells with this woman who had had such an impact on him in so short a time. Meghan, too, could feel the connection between them, and she readily agreed to travel from Canada to Africa to spend a few days under the hot African sun by day and the brilliant African stars by night.

'the stars were aligned ... both felt it was meant to be'

Staying in a tent in 'the middle of nowhere' gave the couple a chance to truly get to know each other. While watching the myriads of stars – which Harry has said were 'aligned' – move across the heavens in the dramatic night sky of that part of the world, a love was starting to grow, a love that both felt was 'meant to be'.

On return to their respective countries, both Meghan and Harry were sure that there was a future for them together, but Harry was nervous. He knew that intense media interest could damage, if not kill, any relationship, particularly one still in its infancy, so the decision was made to keep their new-found love a secret. Of course, if this was to be achieved, a different approach was needed. Not for the high-profile appearances at restaurants, parties and functions; instead, it was to be quiet evenings at home, only made possible by numerous journeys across the Atlantic as their personal work commitments kept them physically on different continents.

Harry and Meghan managed to keep their romance a secret for several months, but inevitably the news leaked out that Harry had a serious girlfriend and the media went into overdrive. In October 2016, Meghan suddenly found herself under a very different spotlight from the one she was more accustomed to as an actress. Her every move was monitored and there was much discussion over her African-

American background, some news commentators considering this a block to her ever having royal credentials. So racist and sexist were the comments that, unusually for a member of the royal family, Harry felt moved to issue a formal statement in which he castigated the attitude of the press towards Meghan and demanded that she be treated with respect, explaining that 'this is not a game, it is her life'.

Fortunately, as a confident 36-year-old woman who knew her own mind, Meghan was able to deal with these unfamiliar pressures and she was not deterred. The media realised it had overstepped the mark and backed off, allowing the couple to continue their long-distance relationship unhindered. Nevertheless, despite the fact their relationship was now public knowledge, over the next few months they continued to keep a low profile, only being seen out together on a few occasions: once in early May 2017 – a year after their first meeting – at the Coworth Polo Club in Ascot, where they shared a kiss, and then later that same month, on the 20th, at the wedding of Pippa Middleton, the sister of Harry's sister-in-law Catherine. On this occasion, Meghan attended the reception only, in order to avoid any potential distraction away from the bride herself on the part of the press.

INVICTUS GAMES

The first public appearance for the couple came at the third annual Invictus Games event held in Toronto in September 2017, conveniently the city that Meghan called home at that time.

Working on the Invictus Games is an important part of Harry's life, and so it was no surprise that he wanted to have his girlfriend, as Meghan was by then, at his side at this major event. Although both were present at the opening ceremony, they were sitting apart. Their first appearance as a couple came early in the week during the wheelchair tennis tournament, leading to much excitement all round as they later strolled, hand in hand and completely relaxed, among the crowds.

It was to be the final evening that left no doubt over their feelings for one another. Initially the couple watched the events from different parts of the stadium, Meghan at one end with her mother Doria Ragland and friends Jessica Mulroney and Markus Anderson, Harry at the other with dignitaries and VIPs.

It was a proud Meghan who watched Harry deliver his moving speech at the end of the Invictus Games when he urged everyone present to take away from their experience some of the Invictus spirit to 'improve something – big or small – in your life, for your family, or in your community … make an Invictus goal for yourselves.' Meghan was able to witness for herself the passion that Harry has for the Games and the hard work and effort that he has put into making them the huge global success that they have become in such a short time.

'the picture was complete'

For the final part of the event, Harry joined Meghan and her mother in the Air Canada suite to watch the closing ceremony, which included performances by Bruce Springsteen, Bryan Adams and Kelly Clarkson. Onlookers noted the strong chemistry between Harry and Meghan and the easy relationship Harry had with Meghan's mother. When Harry was seen to lovingly kiss his girlfriend, the picture was complete – press speculation moved up a gear, from romance to a potential engagement.

A SIMPLE PROPOSAL

Just over two months after the Invictus Games – on 27th November at 10am – the announcement that the country had been waiting for came from Clarence House. Prince Harry and Meghan Markle were engaged to be married.

It may have been only 18 months after their first meeting, but even on first setting eyes on Meghan, Harry knew he had met someone special. Although it had not been the nine-year courtship of Harry's brother William and his wife Catherine the couple had got to know each other well in their 18 months together.

As it had been Harry's aim to keep Meghan out of the public gaze as much as possible, they had spent much time alone in the privacy of their homes, just the two of them, or with close friends, which had helped create a strong, loving bond. It is, therefore, perhaps no surprise that Harry chose an intimate, simple home setting when it came to his proposal of marriage rather than making a flamboyant gesture.

That moment came when the couple were in Harry's home, Nottingham Cottage – the two-bedroom property in the grounds of Kensington Palace – which

Town Crier Tony Appleton outside Kensington Palace after it was announced that Harry and Meghan were engaged

Meghan had moved into just a few weeks previously. The couple were cooking a roast chicken for their evening meal, when Harry dropped to one knee and, with ring in hand, asked Meghan to be his wife. Although taken by surprise by Harry's 'very romantic, very sweet' proposal, Meghan did not make Harry wait for an answer, accepting his proposal almost 'before [he] had finished the sentence'. Meghan was so quick to say, 'Can I say yes now?' that she almost forgot about the ring that Harry was proffering, but the beautiful diamond engagement ring was soon slipped on her finger.

In actual fact, the proposal had come a few days before the official announcement was made. One of the first to know of Harry's intention would have been the Queen herself, as Harry, standing then fifth in line to the throne, first had to ask her permission to marry, in order to comply with the Royal

Marriages Act 1772. The general public were delighted, and both families involved were equally pleased with the news. The Queen and Prince Philip made a formal statement that they were 'delighted for the couple and wish them every happiness', while Harry's father Prince Charles said, 'We're thrilled ... it's marvellous.' Harry's brother William and his wife Catherine said they were excited for the couple and added how much they had enjoyed getting to know Meghan. To have a daughter join the British royal family might have seemed a daunting prospect for Meghan's parents Thomas Markle and Doria Ragland, both of whom are private people, but they responded positively with the words, 'Our daughter has always been a kind and loving person. To see her union with Harry, who shares the same qualities, is a source of great joy to us as parents.'

'Harry chose an intimate, simple home setting when it came to his proposal of marriage'

ROYAL ENGAGEMENT RINGS

When Harry presented Meghan with her engagement ring, she was both delighted by its beauty, and moved by its significance, for not only has it been designed by Harry himself but it also contains three very special diamonds with great sentimental value. The centre stone was sourced by Harry from Botswana, a country loved by the couple and the place where their relationship first became truly established. On either side of that central stone sits a diamond that once belonged to Harry's late mother, Diana. The couple have strongly felt that Diana should be included in some way in their happiness and have stated that the ring helps to fulfil that desire.

This sentiment was also expressed by Harry's brother William when he became engaged to his wife Catherine in 2010. William achieved this by placing on her finger the oval sapphire and diamond engagement ring that had formerly belonged to his mother. Unusually, the beautiful ring, which has a 12-carat blue sapphire in

Prince Harry and Meghan Markle in the Sunken Garden at Kensington Palace on 27 November 2017

Permission to Marry

The Royal Marriages Act 1772 originally set out conditions under which members of the royal family could marry, with the aim of protecting the royal family against any unions that could be detrimental to its standing. The Act gave the sovereign the right to reject an unsuitable marriage, and although this power in itself has never been actively exercised, several couples over the centuries were indirectly affected by a passive lack of consent. Following the repeal of the Act in March 2015, the sovereign's consent is only required for members of the royal family as far as sixth in line to the throne. As a result, although Harry was required to do so, his cousin Princess Eugenie, who is due to marry in October 2018 and was eighth in line to the throne at the time of her engagement, did not have to seek the Queen's permission.

the centre surrounded by 14 solitaire diamonds, was originally bought by Prince Charles from the jeweller Garrard, rather than being custom-made for Diana. Costing a relatively modest £28,000 at the time of its purchase in 1981, the ring is priceless to William and Catherine.

Meghan, however, is not the only member of the royal family to be wearing an engagement ring designed by her husband-to-be. The Queen wears a stunning diamond ring that was created by Prince Philip. This ring features a central three-carat diamond flanked by ten smaller pavé stones and, rather like those given by William and Harry, it has a connection to Philip's mother, containing stones sourced from a tiara worn by his mother Princess Alice of Battenberg on her wedding day. That ring has now been on the Queen's finger for more than 70 years.

Of all the royal engagement rings, it is Camilla's which is deemed to be the most valuable in intrinsic terms, although it also has an interesting provenance in that it once belonged to Charles' grandmother, the Queen Mother. Its central large rectangular stone with three diamond baguettes on either side is a distinctive and unusual style, yet it is easy to wear and has beauty in its simplicity.

Meghan shows off the Welsh gold and diamond ring, designed by
Harry, to the many well-wishers at Kensington Palace

Welsh Gold

Since 1923, for the wedding of Elizabeth Bowes Lyon (the Queen Mother) to the Duke of York (King George VI), royal wedding rings have been fashioned from rare Welsh gold from the Clogau St David's Mine near Dolgellau. Identified by a dragon stamp, this gold is the rarest in the world due to the extremely limited supplies available. The gold remaining from one nugget has created rings for the Queen, Princess Margaret, the Princess Royal, Princess Diana and the Duchess of Cambridge. Wedding rings fashioned from other nuggets of Welsh gold were made for Sarah Ferguson when she married Prince Andrew, and the Duchess of Cornwall when she married Prince Charles.

LEFT: *The engagement of Princess Elizabeth to Lieutenant Philip Mountbatten was announced on 10 July 1947 and the happy young couple are pictured together at Buckingham Palace*

PREVIOUS PAGE TOP: *Prince Charles and his fiancée Camilla Parker Bowles in the grand reception room of Windsor Castle, after announcing they were to marry on 8 April 2005*

PREVIOUS PAGE BOTTOM: *Prince William and Kate Middleton in the state apartments of St James' Palace in London on 16 November 2010, after their engagement was announced*

Harry

THE PEOPLE'S PRINCE

On 15 September 1984, a second son was born to the heir to the throne, Prince Charles, and his wife Diana. Named Henry Charles Albert David, but to be known as Harry, the new baby was a younger brother for Prince William, then aged two, and a fourth grandchild for the Queen and Prince Philip. In the 1950s, at the time of his birth, Prince Charles – Harry's father – had had an upbringing typical of the royalty and aristocracy of the day. He spent limited time with his parents, spending much of his early life in the nurseries of the various royal homes in the company of nannies, and, when it was time to start learning, a private tutor was brought in for home schooling.

That was not the start that Charles and Diana wanted for their children and although, because of their busy lives, they did have to employ nannies – most notably Ruth Wallace, Jessie Webb, Olga Powell and, later, Tiggy Legge-Bourke – they tried to spend as much time as they could with their sons and to give them a normal family life.

They also wanted their boys to mix with other children outside the home, so there was no private tutor for William and Harry; instead, they attended a nursery school local to their home at Kensington Palace: Mrs Mynors' in Notting Hill. There, they flourished in the nurturing environment, learning how to interact socially with the other children and benefitting from the structured routine. Seeing the confident man that Harry is today, it is hard to believe that as a small boy, he was shy and quiet; however, at Mrs Mynors', he was encouraged to come out of his shell so that by the time he started at Wetherby pre-preparatory school, also in Notting Hill, he was a self-assured child ready to learn and be part of school life.

LEFT: *Three-month-old Prince Henry of Wales wearing the royal christening gown after the ceremony in St George's Chapel in 1984*

PREVIOUS PAGE: *Prince Harry takes part in the Sentebale Royal Salute Polo Cup at the Singapore Polo Club in 2017*

He became a popular boy, making many friends, and even forming 'Harry's gang', where his natural talent for leadership came to the fore.

At the age of 8, in 1992, it was time for Harry to take the next big step in his education – boarding school. His parents went to great pains to choose an establishment that had a caring ethos and a homely atmosphere, and they found this at Ludgrove Preparatory School in Wokingham, Berkshire. William was already at the school when Harry arrived, which made settling in much easier for a young boy who was away from home for the first time and missing his parents.

That caring ethos of Ludgrove was soon to be put to the test when, not long after Harry had started at the school, he received the news that his parents were to separate. This was, understandably, a difficult time for him, but the support of the joint headmasters Nichol Marston and Gerald Barber, and Gerald's wife Janet, helped him to accept the situation and understand what had happened. They also helped him to adapt to his new life that was now split between his father's home at Highgrove House, Gloucestershire, and his mother's at Kensington Palace in central London.

'his experience has given him a personal understanding of mental health'

That support was called on once again when, in 1997, Harry's beloved mother Diana was killed in car crash in Paris. Harry, while outwardly putting on a brave face and appearing in control of himself, was inwardly consumed with grief, and he has since admitted that it took him very many years to come to terms with what had happened and to face up to his deepest emotions. His experience has given him a personal understanding of mental health issues, and today he is active in his support for charities working in that field.

TOP RIGHT: *Princess Diana follows Prince William, seven years old, and Prince Harry, five, on Harry's first day at the Wetherby School in Notting Hill, West London*

BOTTOM RIGHT: *Princess Diana with Prince William and Prince Harry at Thorpe Park in 1993*

Harry remained at Ludgrove for six years, excelling at sport and art, until it was time to move on to his secondary education. Again, his parents had broken with tradition when they had chosen Eton College, near Windsor, as the senior school for William, and it was there that Harry would inevitably follow. The boys' father, Charles, and grandfather, Philip, had both been pupils at Gordonstoun in Scotland – a school known for its vigorous and unconventional approach to education. While Philip had flourished there, it had not been to Charles' taste, and it was felt that Eton, which had been attended by Diana's father and brother, offered a more suitable alternative, with the added benefit of being nearer to home.

With its emphasis on sport – some of which, such as Eton Fives and the Wall Game, are unique to the school – it was an excellent choice for Harry and, in due course, he became House Captain of Games, having gained a reputation as being a competitive and formidable opponent at rugby. He also enjoyed the Combined Cadet Force (CCF), which allowed him to undertake all kinds of 'military' activities, such as weapon handling, camping, leadership exercises and close target reconnaissance. He achieved the highest rank of Cadet Officer and had the honour in May 2003 of commanding the Guard of Honour at the CCF Tattoo in front of parents, grandparents, Old Etonians and other school VIPs. His CCF experience was to lay the foundations of his future career.

At 18, Harry left Eton with two A levels – a B in art and a D in geography. His plan was to go on to the Royal Military Academy Sandhurst to train as an officer. However, for the moment, he had had enough of education and, like many young people of that age, he had a yearning to explore the wider world, discover new things and perhaps test himself a little by moving out of his comfort zone. He decided to take a gap year – which, as it turned out, lasted nearly two years.

His first stop was Australia, where he started by cheering on the successful England team in the 2003 Rugby World Cup before moving to a cattle ranch, the Tooloombilla Station, which stretches over 40,000 acres in Queensland, where he spent three months working. From there, in February 2004, he travelled to the small African country of Lesotho, offering support to medics and other professionals dealing with the impact of the AIDS epidemic on the local population.

TOP: *Harry rides his horse Guardsman whilst mustering herd bulls in Tooloombilla, Australia during his gap year*

ABOVE: *A passion forms. Harry surrounded by young children in Lesotho. He has since returned to Lesotho to hand over items from the British Red Cross Lesotho Fund*

LEFT: *Playing football at Eton in a match between the School and a team of Old Boys*

ABOVE: *Prince Charles holds the hand of his son as they view bouquets of flowers left in memory of Diana, Princess of Wales in September 1997 in Balmoral, Scotland*

PREVIOUS PAGE TOP LEFT: *Four-year-old Prince Harry dressed for his nursery school nativity play in 1987*

PREVIOUS PAGE BOTTOM LEFT: *Princes William and Harry join their cousins Princess Eugenie (2nd left) and Beatrice (2nd right) on a ski holiday in Klosters in 1995*

CENTRE TOP: *The Prince and Princess of Wales with their sons on a cycling trip during a holiday in the Scilly Isles*

CENTRE BOTTOM: *Prince Harry, part of the Walking with the Wounded expedition team, tries out an immersion suit on the island of Spitsbergen, in preparation for their walk to the North Pole*

Support for AIDS victims had been an area of interest for his mother, and in Lesotho Harry was able to see the reality of life for AIDS orphans and those children born with the disease. So moved was he by his visit that in 2006, in collaboration with Lesotho's Prince Seeiso, he went on to form the charity Sentebale, which aims to support vulnerable children in Lesotho and Botswana, particularly those affected in some way by AIDS.

His gap year over, it was time to start on a career, which for Harry was to be in the armed forces. His aim was to go on to the Royal Military Academy Sandhurst and for this, in September 2004, he had to take the gruelling four-day physical, mental and aptitude test, which causes many hopefuls to fall at this first hurdle. Fortunately, Harry was not one of them and he started his officer training at Sandhurst in May 2005. To ensure a high calibre of officer graduates, training is necessarily tough and has a high dropout rate, but Harry was determined to succeed, whatever challenge might be thrown at him – whether it was a 36-hour patrol or demanding physical training. It was a proud day when he took part in the passing out parade 11 months later in April 2006, with his grandmother the Queen taking the salute in the Sovereign's Parade.

The following month, Harry joined the Blues and Royals, commissioned as Coronet Wales (the equivalent of second lieutenant) and immediately went to Bovington Camp in Dorset for further training before joining his regiment in Windsor. Soon after this, it was announced that Troop Commander Wales, for that was now his title, would be serving in Iraq and Harry threw himself into preparing for this dangerous and difficult task.

However, it was not to be as it was deemed by his superiors and the government to be an unsuitable assignment, potentially – as a result of 'specific threats' – putting his life and those of his fellow soldiers at 'unacceptable risk'. Harry was bitterly disappointed. He had trained hard and was prepared, but it seemed that frontline action was off-limits for him; that is until December 2007, following an

Prince Harry in the desert in Helmand Province, Southern Afghanistan in 2008

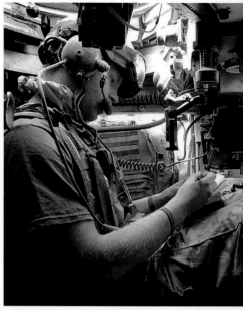

TOP LEFT: *Princes William and Harry play football with children in Semonkong Children's Centre in Lesotho on 17 June 2010*

TOP RIGHT: *Harry sits below the turret of his Spartan armoured vehicle, communicating with other units by radio in Helmand province, Afghanistan in 2008*

RIGHT: *Prince Harry smiles broadly as his grandmother Queen Elizabeth II reviews him and other officers during The Sovereign's Parade at the Royal Military Academy at Sandhurst to mark the completion of their training in 2006*

LEFT: *Prince Harry attending a Service of Remembrance at the Armed Forces Memorial at the National Memorial Arboretum in Staffordshire in 2016*

BOTTOM LEFT: *Prince Harry plants a tree with young orphan Mutsu Potsane, aged 4, at the Mants'ase Children's Home for children in 2004. Mutsu was orphaned by and suffering from Aids near Mohale's Hoek in Lesotho*

BELOW: *Prince Harry lays boots in remembrance during commemorations for the 100th anniversary of the Battle of Vimy Ridge in France in April 2017*

agreement for total secrecy and a media blackout, when concessions were made and he flew to Afghanistan as a forward air controller. Again, things did not go to plan as, after ten weeks, news leaked of his whereabouts and Harry's tour was cut short four weeks early.

He considered his future in the forces and decided he was not ready to leave, so took the decision to train as a helicopter pilot with the view to joining the Army Air Corps (AAC). This entailed yet another tough course, but Harry was found to be a 'natural pilot' and, in May 2010, he was presented with his provisional brevets (or wings) by his father, Prince Charles, the corps' Colonel-in-Chief. Harry then progressed onto an 18-month course, at the end of which, in February 2012, he qualified as an Apache attack helicopter pilot.

Harry now tried again for a deployment in Afghanistan, and this time it was agreed, as long as his presence there did not compromise operational security. He was sent with 662 Squadron to Camp Bastion in Helmand Province, a slightly safer posting than some of the others in that country, where aircrew either provided specific, planned cover for troops or were called out in emergency situations, known as Very High Readiness. It was during this posting that Harry truly 'grew up'; in January 2013, he returned a more mature and deep-thinking person. The boy was gone forever, and he was now his own man.

'the boy was gone forever, and he was now his own man' The experience in Afghanistan had given Harry something else in addition to maturity; he had acquired an understanding of the effects of warfare on military personnel. This knowledge was to later lead him into charitable causes offering support to former members of the forces trying to overcome post-active service disabilities and trauma, whether physical or mental damage, and, in due course, was to result in him setting up the Invictus Games.

Harry left the armed forces in June 2015, but he still needed a sense of purpose and fulfilment. With this in mind, he mapped out a different future for himself, one in which his aim would be to support the causes close to his heart and make a difference to the lives of those less fortunate. He had already set up Sentebale in 2006, and in 2009, along with his brother, the Foundation of Prince William and Prince Harry was established, offering support for a number of charities, but there was more work to do. Harry's specific interests lay in problems facing injured ex-service personnel, deprived and vulnerable children, mental health issues, and conservation – in particular in Africa, a continent for which he has a deep love.

Since then, Harry has played an active part in supporting his chosen charities; his warm and caring personality enabling him to connect with people of all ages, from all walks of life and facing all kinds of problems. While in the army, he had already become involved in this kind of work – in 2011, he had taken part in a gruelling 200-mile sledge expedition to the North Pole in the company of four injured service personnel to help establish the charity Walking with the Wounded (although, unfortunately, Harry's trip was cut short by his need to attend his brother William's wedding).

Unusually for a member of the royal family, he has also spoken openly about his own battles to overcome the grief he had kept bottled inside following the death of his mother, the effects of which at times, he has said, led to him feeling aggressive and often 'very close to a complete breakdown'. It would take him 20 years to seek the counselling that finally helped him come to terms with his loss. It is for this reason that he takes an active interest in mental health charities and, in particular, hopes to see the stigma attached to mental illness become a thing of the past.

In February 2018 Harry was appointed in the Commonwealth headship, a non-political, global role that draws on his charisma and energy. He is expected to highlight the relevance of the Commonwealth to a younger generation, something he has already been involved in. It is a high-profile, high-visibility role in which he will, no doubt, be strongly supported by his new wife.

The Invictus Games

The Games were originally the brainchild of Harry, who has served in the armed forces and has twice been on the frontline in Afghanistan. During his time in the Blues and Royals, he had seen first-hand the effect of warfare on the physical and mental health of service personnel. He also appreciated how sport could help in the rehabilitation of these once active and fit people by re-establishing the senses of self-worth and team spirit, feelings that are often lost when a person suffers a life-changing injury. While on a trip to the United States in 2013, as patron of the charity Landmine Free 2025, Harry had the opportunity to attend the Warrior Games, a sporting event organised by the US Olympic Committee aimed at injured servicemen and women. So impressed was he by the Games that he decided to try something similar in the UK. On his return home, he convinced the Ministry of Defence of his idea and, with the ministry's backing and following months of hard work, he launched the first Invictus Games in September 2014. It was a huge success and was followed by the setting up of the Invictus Games Foundation, which has continued to organise the event since that time. The second Invictus Games was held in May 2016 in Orlando, Florida, and this was followed in September 2017 by a third Games in Toronto.

Meghan

A PRINCESS
FOR OUR
TIME

When news broke that Meghan Markle was Prince Harry's girlfriend, she was largely unknown in the United Kingdom, as indeed she had been to Harry prior to their meeting. An American actress who had for several years played one of the leading parts in the legal drama *Suits*, she was a more familiar figure on that side of the Atlantic. However, since the couple's engagement was announced, public interest in her exploded to a global scale. Her radiant smile and warm, caring personality has led to her enormous popularity and a fascination with discovering exactly who this latest member of the royal family might be, a woman whose influence is beginning to be felt in a variety of areas, from fashion through to serious global issues such as gender and racial equality.

Born on 4 August 1981, Rachel Meghan Markle – known simply as Meghan – is three years Harry's senior. The daughter of Thomas W Markle, a lighting director of Dutch-Irish descent, and African-American psychotherapist Doria Ragland, she grew up in the glitzy surroundings of Los Angeles, California – more precisely the affluent suburb of Woodland Hills that borders the Santa Monica Mountains and lies in the San Fernando Valley. Being relatively near to Hollywood, just under 20 miles (32km) away, with its film and television studios, it is an area popular with celebrities and, as a result, it has excellent facilities and typifies the laid-back Californian lifestyle.

While Meghan, as she grew up, enjoyed all that modern life in California has to offer, her antecedents, on both sides of her family, had had a very different experience. On her father's side, the family had known the hardship of living in a

---

PREVIOUS PAGE: *Meghan greets well-wishers during her first royal visit with Prince Harry to Nottingham in 2017*

RIGHT: *Meghan attends the first Royal Foundation Forum in central London in February 2018*

mining community, travelling from Yorkshire in the UK in 1859 to a new life in the United States. As mining was what they knew, they headed to the Appalachian coal belt, settling in Mahanoy, Pennsylvania, and it was there that Thomas Markle was born in 1945.

Thomas was an ambitious young man and he could not see a future for himself down the mines, so after working in a bowling alley when he left school, he moved to Chicago to become a stage technician in theatre and early television. In time, he became a qualified lighting engineer and set builder, and eventually moved to Los Angeles to work in the flourishing film and television industry in Hollywood. Despite being colour blind – a condition he kept to himself – he went on to be extremely successful, winning an Outstanding Achievement in Design Excellence Emmy for his work on the television shows *General Hospital* and *Married with Children*. Thomas, who is a quiet and private man, is now retired and lives in Rosarito, just over the US border in Mexico, in a clifftop house overlooking the Pacific Ocean.

Thomas married Roslyn with whom he had a son, Thomas Junior, and a daughter, Samantha; however, the marriage soon failed, and some years later he was to meet and marry Doria Ragland, Meghan's mother. Doria, an African-American, has been described by her daughter as a 'free spirit', and Meghan has acknowledged the role that both Doria and Thomas have played in helping her to not only accept her black heritage, but to be proud of it.

Like many black Americans, Doria's ancestors were once slaves in the Deep South. Meghan's great-grandmother Netty Allen grew up in a humble wooden shack in the town of Chattanooga, Tennessee, living in an atmosphere of extreme racial segregation and discrimination where the Ku Klux Klan reigned supreme and racial violence was commonplace.

After the abolition of slavery in the US in 1865, many black people, now free men and women, chose to move to other parts of the country to find work and escape the extreme poverty of the South. The Allens were no different, moving north to the state of Ohio, where in due course Doria was born. The 1960s were a time of huge change, and with the advent of the hippies and flower power, California was the place to be. Doria made the decision to leave Ohio to move to the Golden State to seek her fortune, and it was there in the late 1970s that she met Thomas Markle when she was working as a temp at the studios where Thomas was lighting director. According to Meghan, they were initially drawn together by their 'love of antiques', but whatever the reason, they fell in love and married in 1979, with Meghan being born two years later. Unfortunately, when Meghan was six years old, the couple separated and subsequently divorced, leaving Doria to bring up Meghan as a single mother.

With a determination to better herself, Doria went on to graduate from the University of California in 2016 with a master's degree in social work, and subsequently became a psychotherapist and social worker, specialising in working with the elderly, as well as being a yoga instructor. Meghan has spoken of her closeness to her mother and how her mother raised her to be aware of others who are not so fortunate by taking her to countries such as Mexico and Jamaica to allow her to see for herself the lives of people in impoverished communities.

'be aware of others who are not so fortunate'

Despite the break-up of her parents' marriage, Meghan maintained a good relationship with her father, made easier by her parents' amicable split, and she attributes the many hours she spent in the television studios with him in her young years after school and in the holidays as being the time when the seeds were sown for her acting career. Furthermore, she had seen how hard her parents worked to achieve their goals in life and she knew that if she were to take that same approach, she would one day also fulfil her ambitions.

Meghan attended two private schools: the Little Red Schoolhouse and then the Immaculate Heart High School. She was a diligent student and worked hard at her studies. When it was time to leave, although she knew she wanted to be an actress, she sensibly decided that she should have some qualifications to fall back on, knowing how competitive and difficult an acting career would be. On leaving school, she enrolled at to the Northwestern University School of Communication in Chicago from where she graduated in 2003 with a degree in theatre and international studies. As part of her course, she spent time working as an intern at the US embassy in Buenos Aires. This was an experience that – through the insight it provided into the workings of diplomacy – was to prove useful in future years when she became involved in charitable work.

On leaving university, Meghan still had her sights set on acting, but despite her connections to the film world through her father, in the same way as many other aspiring actresses, she struggled to find work. Not one to give up, she managed to secure a few modelling and short acting roles, supplementing her income by using the calligraphy skills she had acquired at her Catholic school to create handwritten wedding and party invitations – something she has described as her 'pseudo-waitress work', waiting on tables being the usual fill-in work for actors.

'Meghan still had her sights set on acting'

The road to success was a long one and one of her first television jobs was as suitcase girl number 24 on the show *Deal or No Deal*, a game show which involved contestants choosing suitcases to win cash. Although the job entailed little more than smiling, it gave her some valuable exposure and experience in the world of television.

Soon she was appearing in other shows, but this time as an actress, and among these were *General Hospital*, *CSI*, *Without a Trace* and *Castle*. These were relatively minor roles, and her big break came when she landed roles in the films *Remember Me* with Robert Pattinson and Pierce Brosnan, *Get Him to the Greek* with Russell Brand and *Horrible Bosses* starring Jennifer Aniston and Colin Farrell. She also played special agent Amy Jessup in the sci-fi thriller series *Fringe*.

Her acting career was developing, and it was her next – and, as it turned out, last – role that made her name in North America. She played the glamorous paralegal Rachel Zane in the popular Canadian television drama *Suits*, appearing in the show for seven seasons from 2011. Ironically, her last appearance as Rachel saw her character as a bride.

As *Suits* was filmed in Toronto, Meghan left California and made the move north over the border to Canada. It was there that she was to eventually meet Harry – for whom she has given up her acting career to enable her to concentrate on supporting Harry and his charities, while also following and building on causes of her own. Some of those causes focus on gender and race equality; certainly, Meghan has never tried to deny her African-American heritage, rather she has embraced it and is proud of it. Growing up, she experienced several incidents which made her realise that, apart from actual discrimination, there is stereotyping according to race. Often when out with her mother, it would be assumed that Doria, being black, was the nanny and, on one occasion, she was shocked when her mother was verbally racially abused by a driver experiencing road rage.

From her personal point of view, as a mixed-race actress, she found that her complexion was considered too dark for her to be cast as a white woman but not dark enough for a black one, which left her hard to place. Even following her engagement to Harry, she suffered racial slurs from a number of quarters, most notably certain areas of the press, causing Harry to break with royal protocol and issue a statement condemning the behaviour.

Through her background, she has developed an interest in Africa and its problems, and this is something that she shares with Harry, who has often expressed his love of the continent and is involved in several charities in a number of African countries. Also like Harry, Meghan is a supporter of charities that work with disadvantaged young people – in particular One Young World, which seeks to find solutions for various issues facing young people around the world, for which she became a counsellor in 2014. In this capacity, she spoke with authority at the charity's summit in Dublin, speaking on modern-day slavery and challenges relating to the role of women across the globe. As a counsellor, she was in exalted company as previous counsellors have included Kofi Annan, Sir Richard Branson and Archbishop Emeritus Desmond Tutu.

Meghan's other main area of interest is gender equality, and her interest in this topic goes back to when she was just a girl of 11. Incensed by what she saw as a misogynistic advertisement on television that implied a woman's place

'from that moment on, Meghan knew she had a voice'

was in the kitchen, she wrote a letter of complaint to the company involved as well as to several high-profile figures, including the then First Lady Hillary Clinton. Her comments were taken on board and the advert was subsequently changed. From that moment on, Meghan knew she had a voice.

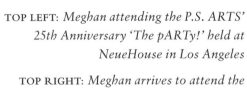

TOP LEFT: *Meghan attending the P.S. ARTS'*
25th Anniversary 'The pARTy!' held at
NeueHouse in Los Angeles

TOP RIGHT: *Meghan arrives to attend the*
Elton John AIDS Foundation's 13th Annual 'An
Enduring Vision' Benefit in New York in 2014

BOTTOM RIGHT: *Meghan played paralegal Rachel*
Zane in the American television series Suits

FOLLOWING PAGE LEFT: *At the 12th Annual CFDA/*
Vogue Fashion Awards in New York in 2015

FOLLOWING PAGE RIGHT: *At the Elton John AIDS*
Foundation Benefit, New York, 2014

ABOVE: *Meghan is shown how to wear a parachute by the soldiers of the 173rd Airborne Brigade during a holiday visit in December 2014 to Vicenza, Italy*

FOLLOWING PAGE ABOVE LEFT: *Meghan with service members during the USO Holiday troop visit at Bagram Air Field in December 2014 in Bagram, Afghanistan*

FOLLOWING PAGE ABOVE RIGHT: *A UN Women ambassador, Meghan discusses gender equality at a UN Women conference in New York on International Women's Day 2015*

RIGHT: *Meghan joins other volunteers, former Chicago Bears linebacker Brian Urlacher, left, and Washington Nationals pitcher Doug Fister for a holiday visit to the crew of the USS Ross in Rota, Spain in 2014*

In later years, as an actress, she saw first-hand how women could be treated in an inferior manner in a male-dominated industry, and she was particularly dismayed by the emphasis placed on personal beauty when it came to a woman being offered a role or being taken seriously.

During that time, she was writing a lifestyle blog website called The Tig, and to tie in with Independence Day, she wrote an article about personal independence. On the back of that post, she was amazed to be invited by the Senior Advisor to the Executive Director of UN Women to work for the organisation as an advocate. It was an opportunity she felt she could not turn down, but she also knew that to do the role as well as she could, she would need to find out more about the UN's work. Her solution was to travel to the headquarters in New York, where she shadowed the UN Secretary General's team. With the confidence that this gave her, she travelled to Rwanda, the country with the highest percentage of women in its parliament, to discover how women were empowering themselves. She was also able to talk to women in towns and villages about the education of girls and their aspirations.

Meghan also used The Tig to voice her opinions on a number of topics, some frivolous and joyful, but others more serious, such as the importance of women using their vote and how making the most of one's appearance is not diametrically opposed to feminism. Meghan showed that she is an independent, modern woman, unafraid of voicing her opinions, while also trying to do some good in the world.

Much of her work will now be focused on the Royal Foundation, of which she is now a patron, but she will also be able to inject her passion into other areas about which she feels strongly on a personal level. This is likely to include issues faced by girls and women beyond those relating to gender equality, with special focus on the problems encountered by females living on the African continent.

It was with some sadness that Meghan decided to close The Tig just before her engagement to Harry, but now with her new royal status, she will find another voice, one that is stronger, bolder and louder and, most importantly, one that will be heard across the world.

Meghan meets the crowds during a visit to Cardiff Castle in 2018

World Vision

World Vision is a charity Meghan has supported
for many years. As an ambassador for World Vision
Canada, in 2016 Meghan travelled to Rwanda to see
the work being done there to bring clean water to
isolated villages. She has since helped to provide
access to water for around 6,700 people in a rural area
of Rwanda. This trip saw her become World Vision's
global ambassador. In 2017 she undertook a learning
trip to girls' projects in India with World Vision.

ABOVE: *Meghan attends the royal family's Christmas Day morning church service in Sandringham, Norfolk in 2017 wearing a Philip Treacy fascinator and a Sentaler coat*

LEFT: *Meghan, wearing a Burberry coat with Strathberry bag, waves to cheering crowds at Edinburgh Castle during an official visit to Scotland in February 2018*

ABOVE RIGHT: *Meghan, wearing a dress and cream coat by Amanda Wakeley and carrying a Mulberry clutch, arrives with Prince Harry for the Commonwealth Service at Westminster Abbey in March 2018.*

FAR LEFT: *Meghan wearing an Alexander McQueen suit as she attends the Endeavour Fund Awards Ceremony with Prince Harry in London in February 2018*

A Royal Power Couple

Meghan is now officially a member of 'The Firm'. Her life will change immeasurably, and she will be bound by some of the conventions and protocol that accompany her royal status. For example, she will be expected to refrain from giving any political opinions – she has in the past been a vocal Democrat in her home country – and to follow royal etiquette rules, which will include, when dining, using cutlery in the English way rather than the more casual American style and adhering to a 'royal' dress code.

For official appearances Meghan will be expected to wear clothes that are modest, and she may be expected to wear a tiara for certain events. However, we know that Harry and Meghan, and, indeed, Harry's brother William and his wife Catherine, are modern royals, and in the coming years there is likely to be a relaxation of some of the rules surrounding the royal code of conduct as they seek to create a monarchy relevant to the changing times.

Harry, of course, has been a popular member of the royal family for many years, but his bride has fast been capturing the hearts of the public, not only in the UK but across the world. According to the search engine Google, her name was the most searched-for term during 2017 as people sought to find out more about her and her activities, while those lucky enough to meet her have spoken about her warm, genuine and welcoming personality. In the months before their wedding, Meghan had the chance to visit some of the regions of the UK to become familiar with the country and its people as she and Harry undertook a number of official appearances. The first of these was to Nottingham just a few days after their engagement was announced where they attended a World AIDS Day hosted by the Terrence Higgins Trust. Being Meghan's first outing as Harry's fiancée, she was under scrutiny, but it was a test she passed with flying colours.

PREVIOUS PAGE: *Harry and Meghan during a visit to Cardiff Castle in January 2018*

Further visits included a trip to Edinburgh in Scotland, Brixton in London, Belfast in Northern Ireland and Cardiff in Wales. At each location, the couple visited local enterprises: in Edinburgh, Social Bite's Home restaurant that supports the homeless; in Brixton, a community youth radio station; in Belfast, tourist attraction Titanic Belfast and the city's dockyards; and in Cardiff, a celebration of Welsh culture in Cardiff Castle, as well as STAR Hub leisure centre that offers sport to disadvantaged children.

Meghan appeared with Prince Harry and the Duke and Duchess of Cambridge at the Royal Foundation Forum in February 2018 where they took to the stage to talk about charitable projects they are involved in currently and their aims for the future under the theme Making a Difference Together. The Foundation was originally set up by William and Harry, who were joined by Catherine after her marriage to William and now by Meghan, who worked behind the scenes of the foundation in the months leading up to her marriage. Similarly, Meghan has joined her husband, brother-in-law and his wife as a patron of Heads Together, the charity that offers support to people living with mental health problems, an area that Harry feels passionate about, having struggled with his own issues following the death of his mother.

Harry has always enjoyed a close relationship with his brother, and with their wives working alongside them, that bond can only grow stronger. Harry has said, 'We are stuck together for ever.' Like William and Catherine, Harry and Meghan have huge appeal and it is this that will give them the power to ensure their messages are heard and, most importantly, acted upon. They have spoken of their desire to make a difference and it will be through the strength of their love for each other, their shared goals and interests, that they will start to create a new style of royal family – one that works for the people with the people.

Wherever the couple appear in public, they are met with warmth and good wishes, such is the affection for them, while Meghan has taken to her new role and life in the limelight with ease and grace. With their shared interests, love and support for each other, and desire to help bring about positive change to the world in so many ways, Meghan and Harry will be a 'power royal couple' of the future who are certain to make a difference to so very many lives.

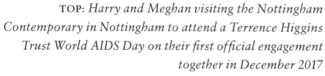

TOP: *Harry and Meghan visiting the Nottingham Contemporary in Nottingham to attend a Terrence Higgins Trust World AIDS Day on their first official engagement together in December 2017*

ABOVE: *The royal couple meet the Shetland pony from the Royal Marines at Edinburgh Castle in February 2018*

TOP CENTRE: *Harry and Meghan meet children on a visit to STAR Hub in Tremorfa, Cardiff in January 2018*

Harry & Megan
Brixton
you

ence
her

ABOVE: *Members of the public wait for Harry and Meghan for their visit to Reprezent FM in Brixton, London to learn about its work supporting young people*

LEFT: *Prince Harry, Meghan Markle and the Duchess and Duke of Cambridge during the first Royal Foundation Forum in central London in February 2018*

PREVIOUS SPREAD: *General view of the Victoria Memorial, which is located at the end of The Mall outside Buckingham Palace, the official residence of the British monarch. Buckingham Palace was originally known as Buckingham House when it was built for the Duke of Buckingham in 1703*

TOP FAR LEFT: *The front facade of Clarence House, the official London residence of Prince Charles and the Duchess of Cornwall*

LEFT: *A general view of Kensington Palace, London, the official residence of Prince Harry and Meghan, The Duke and Duchess of Cambridge and other senior royals*

BOTTOM FAR LEFT: *Highgrove House and gardens, the official country residence of Prince Charles and the Duchess of Cornwall*

BOTTOM CENTRE: *An aerial view of the Queen's Sandringham Estate in Norfolk, where the royal family spend their Christmas holidays*

BOTTOM LEFT: *Balmoral Castle in Aberdeenshire, Scotland, is one of the summer holiday homes for the royal family*

KENSINGTON PALACE

When Meghan and Harry met, Harry was living in the two-bedroom house within Kensington Palace, Nottingham Cottage, known by royals as 'Nott Cott', and it was there that Meghan moved prior to the couple's engagement. With its simple design of two reception rooms, single kitchen and bathroom, and small garden, it makes a cosy starter home for the newlyweds, along with Meghan's two rescue dogs, Guy the beagle and Bogart the Labrador cross, which were shipped over from Canada to be with their owner. However, in time, the couple will need to move to more spacious accommodation, particularly if they start a family as they have indicated is their wish. This could be to the 21-room Apartment 1 that is adjacent to William and Catherine's 20-room Apartment 1A. This was the home of the Duke and Duchess of Gloucester, who had previously offered the apartment to William and Catherine in 2010.

Kensington Palace, which was built by Sir George Coppin in 1605, has a long history as a royal home, its first residents being King William III and Queen Mary II in the latter part of the 17th century. In those days, Kensington was not in the centre of London but was a rural village with open fields; it was thought that this location would benefit the King's health as he was afflicted with chronic asthma. The Palace was called Nottingham House at that time – as reflected in the name of Harry's two-bedroom cottage, Nottingham Cottage, where he and Meghan spent evenings at home during their courtship, as well as being the location for Harry's proposal. William and Mary paid £20,000 for the house – an enormous sum at the time – and they immediately set about altering and expanding the house, as well as landscaping the gardens in the formal Netherlands style that was popular in that era. They moved into the house in 1689, but their residence was a short one as Mary died in 1694 of smallpox, followed by her husband in 1702 after contracting pneumonia. After the deaths of William and Mary, the Palace was further extended and altered by Queen Anne, who took it over. This work was continued by King George I, who spent lavishly on the building both inside and out. The last monarch to use the Palace as a home was King George II; however, following the death of his wife Queen Caroline, he allowed the house to fall into disrepair, and from the date of his death in 1760, the Palace became a residence for less senior royals. It was also divided into large apartments so that several households could live there at the same time. For Harry, Kensington Palace has many childhood memories as it was here that he lived as a boy with his parents, Charles and Diana, in the combined Apartments 8 and 9. Currently, the Palace is home to Harry's brother William, his wife Catherine and their children who live in the refurbished four-storey, 20-room Apartment 1A, which takes up half the Clock Tower wing and was the former residence of William and Harry's great-aunt Princess Margaret.

BUCKINGHAM PALACE

An iconic image of London and Great Britain, Buckingham Palace is probably the most famous of all the royal buildings, known and recognised across the world, and Meghan has already become familiar with it – indeed, it was where she was first introduced to her grandmother-in-law the Queen. The royal ownership of buckingham Palace dates from 1761 when King George II purchased it for his wife Queen Charlotte. Since then, it has become the most important royal residence and has been established as the official London residence of sovereigns from 1837, when Victoria became Queen.

'the most famous of all the royal buildings'

Built in the 1700s as a house, it was transformed into its current neo-classical style by King George IV, who called in the top architect of the day John Nash to alter and extend the building in his signature yellow Bath stone. Later, Queen Victoria further expanded the building with a new wing, which included the now famous balcony upon which the royal family appear for Trooping the Colour and other occasions, such as royal weddings and celebrations of national importance.

Having commissioned the palace wing featuring the balcony, to mark the opening of the Great Exhibition in 1851, Queen Victoria was the first monarch to appear on the balcony of Buckingham Palace. The first newlyweds were Princess Mary (daughter of King George V and Queen Mary) and her husband Henry, Viscount Lascelles in 1922. Twelve years later, in 1934, Prince George, Duke of Kent, and Princess Marina of Greece became the first royals to wave at the jubilant crowds instead of bowing, as had formerly been the custom. The first newlyweds to kiss on the balcony were Harry's parents, Prince Charles and Princess Diana, on 29 July 1981.

While the Queen has an apartment in the Palace, it is also very much a working building with 92 offices and 19 state rooms for welcoming foreign dignitaries and other VIPs; it is also the venue for the Queen's weekly meeting with the prime minister. Buckingham Palace is home to many valuable works of art, and many are on display for visitors to the Palace to enjoy. These include not only numerous paintings – in particular, works by Rubens, van Dyck, Stubbs and Canaletto – but also sculptures, furniture, porcelain, furnishings and photographs. These can be seen in the State Rooms and the Queen's Gallery, which are open to the public, often with specifically themed exhibitions on display, as well as musical recitals, lectures, talks and performance art to be enjoyed. Visitors can also view the Throne Room and the Ballroom, and marvel at the sweeping Nash-designed Grand Staircase that theatrically leads to the State Rooms, with its low wide stairs allowing for dramatic, yet graceful, entrances and exits, and its portrait-adorned walls exuding a sense of history.

HIGHGROVE HOUSE AND CLARENCE HOUSE

Highgrove House in Gloucestershire and Clarence House in London are the residences of Harry's father, Prince Charles. Highgrove, built in 1796 and bought by the Duchy of Cornwall in 1980, represents Charles' country residence and it is his favourite home. Due to his interest in sustainability and environmental protection, he has added many technological features designed to reduce the property's carbon footprint. Thanks to its gardens, woodland and parkland, Highgrove will provide a wonderful private retreat for Harry, Meghan and any children they might have.

Charles' London residence, Clarence House, is familiar to Harry as it was also his home from 2002 until 2012. It is a venue for family gatherings and official receptions and events, and its proximity to Kensington Palace makes it ideal for short informal visits when Harry's father and stepmother Camilla are in town.

SANDRINGHAM AND BALMORAL

Sandringham in East Anglia and Balmoral in Aberdeenshire, Scotland, can be considered as the holiday homes of the royal family. Both are privately owned by the family rather than forming part of the Crown Estate, the former having been bought by Edward VII in 1862 when he was Prince of Wales and the latter by Queen Victoria's husband Prince Albert in 1852 as a Highland retreat.

'an idyllic escape from the bustle of everyday life in London'

Balmoral, with its wild moorland – ideal for walking and outdoor pursuits – and the nearby traditional annual Highland Games at Braemar, is the choice for the summer months. Set in 50,000 acres (20,200 hectares) of Scottish estate, the granite Scottish baronial-style castle, dating from the 15th century, provides an idyllic escape from the bustle of everyday life in London – something that Meghan and Harry are sure to appreciate when they want some much-valued quiet time alone.

Sandringham House, in contrast, sits in 20,000 acres (8,100 hectares) of gentle, flat Norfolk countryside. Despite its Jacobean appearance, it is a relatively modern property having been built between 1870 and 1900 on the site of an 18th-century Georgian house that was demolished. It is Sandringham where the royal family spend Christmas each year, following a traditional family programme of events that includes a service at St Mary Magdalene Church on Christmas Day. Many members of the general public gather in the paddocks at the rear of the building to cheer as members of the family arrive and leave the church.

Meghan has already experienced her first Sandringham Christmas. In 2017, she was invited to join the family for the festive celebrations. Usually, this invitation is only extended to spouses, so her presence was seen as a significant step towards the relaxation of convention. As Harry and Meghan walked arm-in-arm from the church, they chatted to the delighted crowd gathered there, no doubt reflecting that, for their next Christmas, they would be appearing as man and wife.

While Meghan and Harry's marriage is one built on love, respect and shared values, it is also one in which a true partnership is being created in every sense. Following Harry's appointment as Youth Ambassador for the Commonwealth, the couple have made it clear that it is a role they will work within together, helping to support young people in the Commonwealth and allowing their voices to be heard. Indeed, Meghan began her work in this area even prior to her marriage by participating in an official capacity at several events, including a youth forum for young decision makers, a reception to promote global gender equality through girls' education and, in the month before her wedding, the annual Anzac Day commemorative services to mark the contribution made by Australian and New Zealand forces in the First and Second World Wars.

The UK will seek to create even stronger ties with Commonwealth countries and it is within this context that Harry and Meghan will be working, much to the pleasure of Harry's grandmother the Queen, who, on her 21st birthday in 1947 during a trip to South Africa, pledged her commitment to serve the people of the Commonwealth for the rest of her life. This baton will be taken on by Harry's father Charles when he becomes King, and Harry and Meghan's work will provide him with vital support, particularly as 60 per cent of the population of the 53 Commonwealth nations is aged under 30 and a youthful representation by the royal family will be both relevant and beneficial.

It is this passion and determination to make the world a better place for current and future generations that has truly bound the pair together and, in conjunction with Harry's brother William and his wife Catherine, it marks a new direction for the royal family. Over the coming years, the reserved formality of the past will be swept aside in favour of a more open monarchy characterised by an approachability, inclusivity and empathy never before seen; a monarchy that is a perfect fit with modern society, a monarchy truly for the 21st century and beyond.

First published in the United Kingdom in 2018 by
Pitkin Publishing
43 Great Ormond Street
London
WC1N 3HZ

An imprint of Pavilion Books Company Limited

Written by Halima Sadat
The moral right of the author has been asserted.

Edited by Sarah Epton
Picture research by Sophie Nickelson
Design concept by Tokiko Morishama
Layout design by Tatiana Losinska

All photographs by kind permission of
PA Images, including p.103, p.138 (both
photographs) and p.146 (top left) © Doug
Peters/EMPICS Entertainment; p.126
and p.139 (right) © M6027D/EMPICS
Entertainment; p.142 © Isabel Infantes/
EMPICS Entertainment. Photographs on
p.134 bottom right and p.136 and p.137
were provided by Alamy Stock Photo.

ISBN 978-1-84165-806-3

A CIP catalogue for this book is available from
the British Library.

10 9 8 7 6 5 4 3 2 1

Reproduction by Rival Colour Ltd. UK
Printed and bound by G. Canale & C. SpA, Italy

This book can be ordered direct from the
publisher at
www.pavilionbooks.com
Sales and enquiries: +44 (0)20 7462 1500
Email: sales@pavilionbooks.com